Can Architecture be an Emancipatory Project?

Dialogues on the Left

Edited by Nadir Lahiji

Winchester, UK
Washington, USA

First published by Zero Books, 2016
Zero Books is an imprint of John Hunt Publishing Ltd., Laurel House, Station Approach,
Alresford, Hants, SO24 9JH, UK
office1@jhpbooks.net
www.johnhuntpublishing.com
www.zero-books.net

For distributor details and how to order please visit the 'Ordering' section on our website.

Text copyright: Edited by Nadir Lahiji 2015

ISBN: 978 1 78279 737 1
Library of Congress Control Number: 2015943108

A CIP catalogue record for this book is available from the British Library.

Design: Lee Nash

Printed and bound by CPI Group (UK) Ltd, Croydon, CR0 4YY, UK

We operate a distinctive and ethical publishing philosophy in all
areas of our business, from our global network of authors to
production and worldwide distribution.

CONTENTS

Notes on Contributors

Libero Andreotti is Professor of Architecture and Resident Director of the Georgia Tech Paris Program at the Ecole Nationale Superieure d'Architecture de Paris La Villette. An architect and an historian, he holds a Ph.D. in Art, Architecture, and Environmental Studies from M.I.T. His most recent books are *SpielRaum: Walter Benjamin et l'Architecture* (Paris, Editions La Villette 2011) and *Le Grand Jeu a Venir: ecrits situationnnistes sur la ville* (Paris, Editions La Villette 2007). He is also co-author, with Xavier Costa, of *Situationists: Art, Politics, Urbanism* (Barcelona: ACTAR 1997) and *Theory of the Derive and other situationist writings on the city* (Barcelona: ACTAR 1997). His articles have appeared in *October, Lotus International, JAE,* and *Grey Room.*

David Cunningham is Deputy Director of the Institute for Modern and Contemporary Culture at the University of Westminster in London and a member of the editorial collective of the journal *Radical Philosophy,* as well as on the International Advisory Board of *CITY: Analysis of Urban Trends, Culture, Theory, Policy, Action.* He is an editor of collections on Adorno (2006) and photography and literature (2005), as well as of a special issue of the *Journal of Architecture* on post-war avant-gardes. Other writings of his on aesthetics, modernism and urban theory have appeared in publications including *Angelaki, Architectural Design, Journal of Visual Culture, New Formations* and *SubStance.* He is currently completing a book on the concept of the metropolis.

Peggy Deamer is Assistant Dean and Professor of Architecture at Yale University. She is a principal in the firm of Deamer, Architects. She received a B.Arch. from The Cooper Union and a Ph.D. from Princeton University. She is the editor of *The Architect as Worker: Immaterial Labor, the Creative Class, and the Politics of Design* (forthcoming, Bloomsbury Press), *Architecture and Capitalism: 1845 to the Present* (Routledge), *The Millennium*

House (Monacelli Press), and co-editor of *Building in the Future: Recasting Architectural Labor* (MIT Press) and *BIM in Academia* (Yale School of Architecture) with Phil Bernstein. Recent articles include "The Changing Nature of Architectural Work" in *Design Practices Now Vol II, The Harvard Design Magazine* no. 33; "Detail Deliberation" in *Building (in) the Future: Recasting Labor in Architecture*; "Work" in *Perspecta 47*; "Practicing Practice" in *Perspecta 44*; and "Design and Contemporary Practice" in *Architecture from the Outside*, Dana Cuff, John Wriedt, eds. Her research examines the nature of architectural work/labor and subjectivity. She is the organizing member of the advocacy group, The Architecture Lobby.

Nadir Lahiji's recent edited books include *The Missed Encounter of Radical Philosophy with Architecture* (Bloomsbury, 2014 and 2015); *Architecture Against the Post-Political: Essays on Reclaiming the Critical Project* (Routledge, 2014); *The Political Unconscious of Architecture: Re-Opening Jameson's Narrative* (Ashgate, 2011 and 2012). He has contributed chapters to numerous books, including *Architecture Post Mortem: The Diastolic Architecture of Decline, Dystopia, and Death*, eds. Donald Kunze, Charles David Bertolin, Simone Brott, (Surrey: Ashgate, 2013); *Architecture and Violence*, edited by Bechir Kenzari, (Barcelona: Actar, 2011), *Spielraum: W. Benjamin et L'Architecture*, edited by Libero Andreotti (Paris: Éditions de la Villette, 2011); *Walter Benjamin and Architecture*, edited by Gevork Hartoonian (London: Routledge, 2010). He has contributed a number of essays to journals including *Architecture Theory Review* and *International Journal of Zizek's Study*.

Joan Ockman is Distinguished Senior Fellow at the University of Pennsylvania School of Design. She is currently also a visiting professor at Cooper Union and Cornell University. She directed the Temple Hoyne Buell Center for the Study of American Architecture at Columbia University from 1994 to 2008. She has written widely on the history, culture, and theory of modern and contemporary architecture. Her book publications include *Architecture Culture 1943-1968* (1993), *The Pragmatist Imagination: Thinking about Things in the Making* (2000), and *Architecture School: Three Centuries of Educating Architecture in North America* (2012). She began her career at the Institute for Architecture and Urban Studies in New York in 1976 and was an editor of its journal *Oppositions* and of the Oppositions Books series.

Erik Swyngedouw is Professor of Geography at Manchester University. His research interests include political-ecology, urban governance, democracy and political power, and the politics of globalization. He was previously Professor of Geography at Oxford University and held the Vincent Wright Visiting Professorship at Science Po, Paris, 2014. His recent publications include *In the Nature of Cities* (co-edited with Maria Kaika and Nik Heynen (Routledge, 2005), *The Post-Political and its Discontents: Specters of Radical Politics Today* (co-edited with Japhy Wilson (Edinburgh University Press 2014). His new monograph, *Liquid Power: Nature, Modernity and Social Power*, was published by MIT Press in 2015.

Introduction

Nadir Lahiji

Instead of singing the advent of the ideal of liberal democracy and of the capitalist market in the euphoria of the end of history, instead of celebrating 'the end of ideologies' and the end of the great emancipatory discourses, let us never neglect this obvious macroscopic fact, made up of innumerable singular sites of suffering....

Jacques Derrida, *Specters of Marx*

The dialogues presented here reflect a simple but urgent question: *Can architectural discourse rethink itself in terms of a radical emancipatory project, and if so, what would be the contours of such a project?* We began from a firm conviction that academic discourse today continues to be blind to the new *emancipatory hypothesis* advanced by the contemporary politico-philosophical radical Left. The liberal intellectual wing of the critical establishment—including many former 'radicals' who like to speak about the 'end of criticality'—has embraced neo-liberalism with a jubilant, almost manic enthusiasm for the post-critical, the post-historical, the post-political, and the post-ideological. This new triumphalism presents itself as 'progressive'. By shutting out all evidence to the contrary, by removing architecture from any larger critique of capitalism and its cultural logic, by forcing out all recalcitrant elements, it has drained the force of radical critique and sacrificed architecture to the neo-liberal order.

A vain cult of 'professionalism' has displaced not only the utopian horizons of the radical Left that were an integral part of architectural debates in the 1960s and early 1970s, but also the much more limited idea that architecture might articulate *any* progressive critical position. As Maurizio Lazzarato notes, a philosophy of the 'virtual' has been corrupted into the 'virtuality' of finance capitalism and credit.[1] And 'virtual architecture', lending itself to this corruption, is sold as a hot commodity of digital capitalism.

Much as the thinking in architectural circles, beginning with the late 1970s, served to discredit any project of radical social change, so the liberal-left wing of the academy today treats any appeal to emancipatory ideas as unrealistic and nostalgic. If this permanent anti-utopianism goes against the revolutionary ideals of the '68 generation, it can also be seen as a perverse fulfillment of them. As Alain Badiou noted recently, 'we are commemorating May '68 because the real outcome and the real hero of '68 is unfettered neo-liberal capitalism. The libertarian ideas of '68, the transformation of the way we live, the individualism and the taste for *joiussance* have become a reality thanks to postmodern capitalism and its garish world of all sorts of consumerism.'[2] This deeper betrayal compels us to ask, once again, what historical agent offers a possibility of emancipation, and where is it located in the urban, social, and architectural reality of today? Moreover, who is the architectural subject? What is the *object* of architecture to which this subject must *be subjected*? And, what is the relationship between a historical agent and architectural *disposifis*?

The cultural discourse of contemporary architecture happily abets the grand 'utopian' project of neo-liberalism's subjection of all social forms to the logics of 'the market'. At the same time, the high institutions of culture have elevated architecture to the status of a 'high art' on the one hand, and a branch of the 'culture industry' on the other, and have propagated and packaged its aestheticization and spectacularization in theory and in practice. Contemporary architecture lends its service to the cultural logic of this order and its economic imperatives to extract the *surplus-value* it needs to reproduce and expand. In this way, a new and powerful fetishism has taken hold of design.

The question of Emancipation is not separable from the

problematic of the Enlightenment and its dialectics. If the Enlightenment was about iconoclasm, contemporary architecture arguably marks a counter-Enlightenment turn towards new forms of *idolatry*.

From this perspective, contemporary architecture seems to be all about the *surfaces* of culture and its *re-enchantment* as commodity form. It operates in the same general domain that Siegfried Kracauer explored in the 1920s in such essays as 'The Mass Ornament' and 'Photography,' and his exploration of the mundane, everyday spaces of the 'hotel lobbies', 'dancing', 'arcades' and Tiller-Girls of the Weimar era.[3] As Thomas Levin in his excellent introduction to *The Mass Ornament* notes, Kracauer used his architecturally trained eye to pursue a utopian moment through the 'revelation of the negative' in the dialectic of Enlightenment.[4] With a 'revolutionary nihilism' similar to Benjamin's, he explored these surface manifestations in order to overcome them. Suspending the traditional opposition between 'applied ornament' and 'functional structure,' Kracauer 'recast the geometry of the mass of Tiller-Girls as both ornamentation of function and functionalization of ornament', as Levin remarks.[5] For him, 'the geometry of human limbs' was at the same time a *mise-en-scène* of disenchantment. As Kracauer wrote: 'The structure of the mass ornament reflects that of the entire contemporary situation. Since the principle of the *capitalist production process* does not arise purely out of nature, it must destroy the natural organisms that it regards either as a means or as resistance.'[6] Kracauer spoke, in this way, of a 'capitalist *Ratio*' that 'flees from reason,' adding prophetically that '*Reason* does not operate within the circle of natural life. Its concern is to introduce truth into the world.'[7] 'It is the *rational and empty form* of the cult, devoid of any explicit meaning.'[8] As Levin explains, 'it is thus in the context of a struggle between *Ratio* and reason that the status of the surface took a new significance.'[9]

Kracauer wrote his essays while reflecting on the notion of

history itself as a process of disenchantment—he used the words 'demythologizing' and disenchantment interchangeably—in distancing himself from the 'will-to myth' in the critique of the Enlightenment. Today, more than ever since the 1920s, we are faced with new mass ornaments and new phantasmagorias in which 'the ornamentation of function and functionalization of ornament' converge, more insidiously than they did in Kracauer's day, but with the same mythologizing effects that for Kracauer eclipsed the 'truth of reason.' It seems that in the context of high-tech capitalism, 'reason' has lost its battle to the winning capitalist *Ratio*.

Today, the surface manifestations of culture have become all-pervasive. Under the ruthless 'rationalizing' bondage of current capitalist *Ratio*, the mythic traits of abstract rationalism and the *re-enchantment* of culture have gone beyond what Kracauer's critique of Enlightenment could have imagined. In architecture, radical critics on the left have been disarmed by a liberal-left academic discourse that misses no opportunity to *affirm*, conveniently and opportunistically, the very gap that was opened with the defeat of the politics of May '68. In this situation, it is imperative that committed theorists take up the task of radical thinking along the lines of what Slavoj Žižek has called 'struggling theory', by posing the question of emancipatory politics.

Although the contributors to this book do not presume to speak on behalf of radical left intellectuals everywhere or anywhere, they nevertheless profess an alliance to an emancipatory politics against the endgame of capitalist 'deterritorialization' and 'fluidification'—in Žižek's words, 'the gnostic-digital dream of transforming humans themselves into virtual software that can reload itself from one hardware to another.'[10] Today, zealous apologists of this digital utopia are legion, especially in architecture schools. We hope this book will help to recast the terms of architectural critique by opening the forbidden question of 'emancipation' in a self-conscious and responsible way.

In the spirit of Žižek's 'struggling theory', four invited critics (or Interlocutors) were asked to pose five questions each, related to the overall theme of architecture and emancipation. Acting somewhat as a moderator, I selected three from each list and circulated them among the participants. Two rounds of responses were thus generated. In the first, each Interlocutor addressed the questions she or he received. The results were then circulated among the participants and each was asked to respond to the others. I assumed the role of coordinator, facilitating communication between the interlocutors—all the while urging them to be provocative in critically articulating their points of view in relation to each other and emphasizing the larger challenge of theory as it might be posed from the position of the Left. I asked them to interrogate the ideologies, opinions, beliefs, myths, fantasies that underlie the present-day hegemonic discourse within the academy, including the claims to a new condition, whether post-critical, post-ideological, post-political and/or post-historical. Joan Ockman was later invited to join the project and agreed to read all the responses and write an 'afterword'. I added my contribution at the end of the collection. My intervention is not intended to offer any 'conclusion.' It stands alone as a dialogue with myself.

I would like here to thank the contributors who took a significant risk by accepting my invitation and for going along with the project's provocative format. I specially thank Libero Andreotti and David Cunningham for reading the early draft of this introduction and offering their editorial insights with valuable suggestions. I am also grateful to Joan Ockman for her valuable addition to this collection.

Questions

The followings are the questions each interlocutor wanted to address to the others that formed the basis of the subsequent dialogues in the book. Each interlocutor originally posed five questions from which three major ones were selected.

Questions from Libero Andreotti

I. What "basic banalities" or truisms might help reconstitute a genuine architecture of the Left today? Are the critiques of commodity fetishism, of ideology and institutions still effective weapons in an age of global digital capitalism? What would a partisan, militant Left historiography of modernism look like?

II. Is there a sense in which progressive architectural theory in the US from the late 1970s onward shares some responsibility for the recent post-political turn? How did ostensibly critical political positions evolve from the 1980s to the present? What ambiguities, blind spots, or omissions helped prepare the way for the so-called "New Pragmatism"? For example, did the continual spurning of economic determinism and vulgar Marxism in the discourse of Jameson and others (not to mention the mantra of Modernism's "failed utopias") inhibit debate on the actual forces that were massively reshaping the city and the profession, including the traditional relationship between architects and developers? In what way did the theoretical disavowal of political activism minimize concern for the seemingly mundane issues of justice and democracy within the workplace, promoting the elitist celebrity culture that would generate a new cycle of commodification?

III. Wittingly or not, did a certain fatalistic Tafurianism encourage the rise of a politically aloof architectural *realpolitik* that would, in the writings of his self-proclaimed followers, uncritically embrace technocratic neo-liberalism? How was the use of star designers in massive speculative building campaigns that benefit developers of the "innovation economy" implicitly sanctioned by progressive theory from the 1980s onwards? How was Tafuri's critical discourse understood and used by Michael Hays and others within the emerging field of HTC in academia (History, Theory, Criticism)? What doctrinal assumptions, taboos and exclusions operated to displace Marxist theory from a political to a formal and aesthetic plane? How did the theoretical discourse on digital design respond (or fail to respond) to the aggressive corporate re-engineering of design into an impersonal self-organizing process that effectively subordinates architecture to optimizing "parameters" with no other ambition than to build more for less?

Questions from David Cunningham

I. Famously, Manfredo Tafuri argued that in seeking to articulate any conception of architecture *qua* architecture as an 'emancipatory project' it was first crucial to identify precisely those historical "tasks which capitalist development has taken away from architecture." To what extent does this remain a necessary task today? And, if so, how do you think that this changed in the nearly half a century since Tafuri wrote this?

II. Whether directed against the Leninist model of the vanguard party or against socialist and social democratic forms of statism, the centre of gravity of radical politics has apparently shifted very much towards an insistence upon the necessity and capacity for political change to be directed from the "bottom up." This raises the obvious question: how far is it possible to conceive of architecture as anything other than a 'top down' process? How open can the forms and practices of architectural (or building) production be to a "refunctioning" in more collective, "horizontalist" and/or "democratic" terms? Might new computer technologies play a part in this? And should we take it for granted that this is, in fact, a necessary condition of any progressive conception of architecture as an emancipatory project today?

III. In their controversial sociological account of a so-called "new spirit of capitalism," Luc Boltanski and Eve Chiapello seek to trace the recuperation of earlier leftist and counter-cultural demands for "liberation" within contemporary neo-liberal politics and managerialism. For architecture and urbanism, this can perhaps be seen most clearly in the fate of both theoretical critiques of urban planning and bureaucratic welfarism—from Lefebvre and the Situationist International to post-autonomia—and the practical strategies pursued by, say, 'right to the city' social movements and squatter groups born of the late 1960s, in which, arguably, opposition to an earlier moment of capitalist development now finds itself recuperated as a model of self-organized entrepreneurship, and may even be deployed to legitimize neo-liberal demands to roll back the state and "big government." How far would you accept such an account? And, if you do, to what extent might this be understood to ineliminably 'compromise' the underlying assumptions of much would-be radical architecture today?

Questions from Peggy Deamer

I. Has the discourse of globalization harmed, usurped, or displaced architecture theory's critical agenda? In *After Globalization*, Eric Cazdyn and Imre Szeman suggest that globalization has damaged the Marxist agenda because of its, and along with it, capitalism's, seeming inevitability. Is there 1) merit to this observation and 2) evidence of its unintended or intended negative effects in radical architectural theory?

II. Theories of architectural autonomy, particularly as they are presented in the Anglo-American context, valorize architecture's divorce from politics and the economy. Is there, as some like K Michael Hays and Pier Vittorio Aureli would have it, any hope for a radical agenda within the discourse of autonomy?

III. The understanding of architecture as immaterial labor (for its being design) and the architect as a member of the creative class situate the discipline within (what is characterized as) the "knowledge economy." Is there evidence that the knowledge economy functions differently than capitalism as we have traditionally understood it and if so, is an emancipatory architectural discourse to be found in it?

Questions from Erik Swyngedouw

I. If emancipatory transformation necessarily implies a form of creative destruction, how can we deal with the violent moment that is inscribed in any process of geographical change?

II. "Nature does not exist!" If we take Žižek seriously on this, what is the place of the non-human in emancipatory urban practices and politics?

III. What, if anything, can radical planners and architects learn from the 'insurgent architects' that have animated so much of urban rebellions in recent years?

Dialogues: Round One

1

Autonomy's Adventures: or What Does it Mean to Politicize Architecture?

Libero Andreotti

It might be said that a chiasmus has emerged recently in one of the longest-running debates in architectural theory: from the autonomy of *architecture* that was the almost obsessive preoccupation of so much post-modernist writing, one has passed, with a recent book by Pier-Vittorio Aureli, to the architecture of *autonomy*.[1] This reversal, or shift in perspective, brings the hyper-politicized discourse of the Italian movement *autonomia* back into a conversation over a term—autonomy—that some among today's "new pragmatists" had already consigned to indefinite retirement.[2]

But is the figure of speech that Fredric Jameson once called the Marxist trope *par excellence* just a rhetorical ploy, a redundant pleonasm designed to uselessly prolong the debate, or is it actually capable of generating the disjunctive shifts the chiasmus has rightly become famous for in the writings of Marx, Benjamin, or Debord? The long answer to this question would depend on whether the ideas advanced by Italian workerists—on the immateriality of work, the centrality of the working class, and the essentially reactive character of capitalism—might offer a plausible framework to understand some of the major developments that have taken place in the field of architecture over the last four decades. Such an analysis, important as it is, is beyond the scope of this essay. What might be worth trying, instead, is a more general reflection on how the chiasmus *itself* might work to reshape the conversation around the scope and limits of autonomy, and the possibility of critical work more generally.[3]

For Debord, the particular type of chiasmus under consideration here, called the "reversed genitive," was nothing less than "an expression of historical revolutions distilled into a form of thought." Hegel had made it the basis of his epigrammatic style, and Feuerbach, alongside other left Hegelians, had used it to mount a devastating critique of Christianity. The unmatched master in the use of the chiasmus, however, had been the young Marx, who in *The Poverty of Philosophy* (a chiastic inversion of Proudhon's *The Philosophy of Poverty*) had made the chiasmus into the principal rhetorical trope for an "insurrectionary" style of argument that, according to Debord, "restored all the subversive qualities of concepts that have congealed into respectable truths." The Situationist technique of *detournement* was itself heavily indebted to the chiasmus for the way it sought to achieve both a conceptual reversal and an active diversion of accepted truths towards new forms of revolutionary practice.[4]

Today, it is an open question whether *any* conceptual reversal *within* architectural theory could seriously make such lofty claims. Even so, some of the possibilities inherent in Aureli's reversal seem worth pursuing. To this end, a few points on political context, obvious as they may be to some, are essential.

Since the election of Ronald Reagan to the presidency in 1980, no discipline has been immune to the deeply corrosive effects of the neo-conservative ideology he ushered in. As Paolo Virno notes, Reaganism was much more than a right-wing reaction. Across the world, its material effects were closer to those of a "revolution in reverse."[5] A "long state of emergency" that "went to the root of things and worked methodically," leaving nothing unchanged, Reaganism not only dismantled the Welfare State, strengthening what Pierre Bourdieu called the "right hand" of government (its military and policing functions) over the "left hand" of its social programs, but invested massively in propagandizing, through every available means and with an unprecedented power of penetration, an extreme anti-statist market fundamentalism designed to discredit any political alternative, in the workplace above all, but also, and more insidiously, in the places where public opinion and cultural attitudes were formed. In the United States, the widespread imposition of neo-conservative doctrine had two major effects on architectural discourse. One was to initiate a long decline in the social awareness inherited from the 1960s. Given theory's investments in that radical critique, this process was reflected in the changing position of theory in many schools and critical venues where, hemmed in by the taboos and prohibitions imposed by the corporatized structure of university departments and cultural establishments like the MOMA in New York, critical discourse came to display an increasingly passive and almost *reverential* character reminiscent of the polite conversation of an eighteenth century salon. The other major effect was a cultural transformation for which the best comparison, for me, would be the movement of "hermeticism" in the 1930s—a term used to describe the mechanism of containment whereby social and political critique are driven underground and made to resurface on a purely aesthetic level. In the US, this was especially apparent in the conflicted formal language of deconstruction and its politically resonant, but materially ineffectual, forms of argument and address. In architecture schools and elsewhere, deconstructivism's aestheticisation of politics resulted in a characteristic mode of theorizing that Debord called "lateral critique," a stance "which perceives many things with considerable candour and accuracy, but places itself to one side. Not because it affects some sort of impartiality—for on the contrary it must seem to find much fault—yet without ever apparently feeling the need to reveal a *cause*, to state, even implicitly, where it is coming and where it wants to go."[6] Elsewhere, in what can now be seen as an effort to defuse, and then to disarm the critical force of theory, Debord would compare this type of discourse to a "weapon without a trigger." Critical theory's final demise, however, came

4

with the emergence of the overtly managerial and pop-marketing discourses that began to dominate architectural debates under the term "new pragmatism" in the early 2000s.

It is beyond the scope of this essay to consider the extent to which the discourse of *autonomia*—in the peripheral but symbolically central context of Italy from the 60s onward—might itself have been an effect of similar changes rather than a clear-headed analysis of them. Undeniably, however, the autonomists did at least attempt to theorize the massive dislocations brought on by Reaganism and the so-called post-Fordist economy within an overall perspective of political emancipation, and this is certainly what gives force to Aureli's chiasmus. Put simply, the shift from "the autonomy of architecture" to "the architecture of autonomy" opens the possibility of a movement outward and against the aestheticizing trend of the last four decades, towards a re-politicization of architecture that might reconnect with a long-suppressed utopian tradition of radical critique that was a central feature of Modern Architecture from the start.

The most obvious precedent for such a movement (it is significant that Aureli's book appeared after 2008) were the vast public building campaigns that were realized—in an astonishing variety of forms—in the aftermaths of the two World Wars, the Russian Revolution, and the Great Depression.[7] Their remains— some brilliant, others crude or confused if well meaning—still make up a good part of the urban fabric of cities from Paris to Vienna to Amsterdam and New York. The product of socialist administrations, they issued from a tradition of enlightened political thinking that, as Vidler makes clear, formed the intellectual context for Emil Kaufmann's *Von Ledoux bis Le Corbusier* (1933), which first popularized the idea of autonomy among architectural theorists. Indeed, a left-wing, utopian, anti-fascist impulse was central to much of the debate over autonomy all the way up to the 1970s. Aldo Rossi's writings, for example, carried forward Kaufmann's Jacobin rationalism, stressing as much the autonomy of form as the wider ethico-political project of autonomy developed by Raniero Panzieri in the early years of Italian workerism.[8]

In the US, however, the drive to extinguish all remnants of radical politics from Modern Architecture in what Reinhold Martin has rightly called a vast project of "unthinking utopia" tended automatically to privilege a very particular and for architectural theory until then marginal tradition of formal autonomy developed by Colin Rowe and his student Peter Eisenman. Like any specialized area of activity, architecture was held to be bound to an internal investigation and transformation of its own language. The assertion of a disciplinary "specificity" centered on the question of form served to claim a margin of action against 'external' forces that (whether in the form of deterministic theories of design or as powerful pressures from the world of business or politics) were felt to threaten architecture's integrity as a discipline. In Eisenman's more intransigent version, this tradition simply equated autonomy with self-referentialism, thus bringing the discourse of autonomy in line with an art for art's sake tradition that was always deeply rooted in the romantic Ayn Randian view of architecture in the US. This return to (or persistence of) nineteenth century aestheticism, though disguised in avant-gardist terms recalling the critique of representation in the arts, resulted in the characteristic stance of elitist condemnation of utilitarianism and philistinism that echoed through much of the American discourse of autonomy, borrowing from Adorno, Popper, and many others to target commercialism, 'vulgar Marxism,' and all things 'ideological.'

In practice, of course, such principles were hard to reconcile with the globally expanding business enterprises that, beginning in the late 80s, occupied many of autonomy's one-time proponents. Eisenman himself made the point painfully clear in a recent lecture to Edinburgh architects when he declared:

There are pressures being put on all of us. They say, "We want your signature on our shopping mall." Do I know what to do? I don't. I want to work, like everyone else. I'm not certain, and I want to be forgiven by all of you for trespassing into the world of commerce! The rhetoric of modernism has gradually become the rhetoric of capital.[9]

But of course "the rhetoric of modernism" did not undergo this transformation all by itself. None of it would have been possible without the active participation of designers, theorists, and critics. Eisenman's belated contrition suggests instead a feeling of bitter victory—of success gained dishonestly—that is not without relevance for the present-day interest in an architecture of autonomy, as opposed to the autonomy of architecture.

From a left perspective, Aureli's chiastic reversal has at least three obvious advantages. The first is its wide political scope: by shifting the focus of attention from the internal exploration of language to an "outside" of architecture, it foregrounds the need for alternative forms of practice beyond the corporate, neo-liberal business model that is now enshrined in architectural education. The second is that it undermines the validity of a purely aesthetic notion of autonomy of the sort proposed by Eisenman but also practiced, to a significant degree, by more nuanced theorists like Michael Hays. Third, it discredits one of the most pernicious tendencies in US theoretical discourse, which is the habit of opposing autonomy on the one hand with political commitment on the other.

These advantages are not negligible. In my view, they open up a series of useful questions that might serve to revitalize architectural criticism.

One obvious question relates to the variety of possible alternative practices. Here I would simply point to two useful sources for anyone seriously interested in taking up the challenge. One is the early writings of the *Tendenza*, where Rossi and others developed a critical discourse on "the ideology of profession-alism"—namely, the laissez-faire practices of an older generation of "humanist" architects (Zevi, Quaroni) implicated—or so they claimed—in some of the worst excesses of Italy's post-war building boom. Bonfanti's writings, in particular, sought to address through a variety of architectural as well as legal, political and financial means the rampant speculation and class imbalances of cities like Milan, developing criteria that are still cogent in the present-day context. One aspect of this discourse was a renewed focus on the pre-conditions of design and on design itself as the most direct, de-aestheticized expression of those conditions—an orientation towards the 'what' rather than the 'how' reflected in a conscious *deskilling* of design itself in a challenge to the technical specialistic discourse of a degraded professionalism.

The second source is the writing of Gar Alperovitz, especially *America Beyond Capitalism*,[10] which offers an abundance of infor-mation on cooperative arrangements like community devel-opment corporations and land trusts, and as well as the financial instruments currently being used in hundreds of community–based urban design proposals that exist outside of, or hidden beneath, the grand narrative of US corporate archi-tecture. Any serious effort to develop an architecture of autonomy, in my view, would have to be based on new institu-tional foundations such as those described by Alperovitz as based on the principle of a democratization of capital, without which autonomy is bound to remain an essentially defensive and ultimately declining political posture.

A second set of questions are more conceptual. They mainly consist in challenging the narrow empirical framework on which the Anglo-American tradition of formal autonomy is based. In different ways, the main proponents of autonomy in the US today, including Stanford Anderson and Michael Hays, both follow the art-historical tradition that goes from Wölfflin to

Wittkower to Rowe—a tradition with a strongly limiting empirical commitment to the here and now. The effects of this art-historical and connoisseurial approach can be seen, for example, in the *methodological* emphasis both Hays and Anderson place on autonomy as a general principle valid for *all* theoretical and practical work. Configuring autonomy as a *fact*, rather than a *value*, however, radically undercuts the critical, utopian potential of autonomy as a project, allowing Hays, for example, to describe Hannes Meyer's League of Nations project as just as much an example of architectural autonomy as Mies's Seagram Building—despite the vastly different political orientations of these two works.[11] A similar *hypostatization* of autonomy is reflected in the way Hays invokes Adorno's defense of autonomy to affirm the ineluctability of architecture's reification while downplaying the radical utopian tension that was absolutely central to Adorno's efforts to distinguish what he called "authentic art *that takes on itself the crisis of meaning,* from a resigned art consisting literally and figuratively of protocol sentences."[12] In contrast to the generally ecumenical approach to autonomy practiced by Hays and others in the US, the notion of autonomy as a *project* would offer a sharper critical framework from which to evaluate the critical meaning of works, beyond their simple assertion of relative independence vis-a-vis their context. This would also lead to re-evaluating the historiographical categories of success and failure through which some groups of works achieve canonical status while others are simply removed from history books. To understand what such a revision would entail one has only to think of the treatment accorded to the publicly funded housing projects built in Europe in the 1920s, and to their extensions in the urban renewal schemes built in the US after World War II. Up for reconsideration in this sense would certainly be the most symbolic of these projects, Pruitt Igoe, built in Saint Louis in 1954 and destroyed in 1972 amidst a near-universal consensus about the "failure" of government-sponsored public housing.

Pruitt-Igoe, in fact, would be a good case study against which to test the third main advantage of stressing autonomy as a political project. For nothing has been more damaging to the US discourse on autonomy than the pretense of being a-political. The Cold Warrior role that Colin Rowe objectively assumes when his scorn for the utopian dreams of the Modern Movement that Pruitt-Igoe represented is placed side by side with the far more harmful and politically destructive effects of "actually existing American capitalism's" total re-engineering of life through suburbanization should be a reminder, if any is needed, of the fundamental dishonesty of assuming the political neutrality of any discussion of architectural form. Compared to this, Adorno's notion of autonomy as *preliminary* to political engagement—frustrating as it is—will always be preferable. An architecture of autonomy, however, would cut through Adorno's layers of mediation and reflexivity by demanding, with considerably less philosophical introspection, an explicit commitment to a project of political change.

If these are some of the most obvious consequences of following through with the chiasmus opened up by Aureli, what might one say about his own pedagogical practice as evidenced, for example, in a recent collection of studio work entitled *Rome: the Center(s) Elsewhere*? [13] The great strength of the proposal, in my view, is its clear political framework. The project advances a "common interest" approach to urban design that rejects neo-liberal policies of slash-and-burn privatization. In a refreshing break from the depressing free-market discourse, Aureli presents an ambitious scheme for long-term infrastructural improvements that effectively *inverts* neo-liberalism's urban commodification strategies by placing a political program ahead of any market mechanism.

Yet Aureli's proposal is also deeply ambiguous, its progressive programmatic character conflicting with an hypnotic imagery of a post-Fordist work. What we are offered is a stern, almost Hilberseimer-like "contemplation of destiny" that does not so much critically reconfigure the new spaces of post-Fordist production as it distills and generalizes them to an extreme degree. Indeed, with only a few slight changes relating to the "immaterial" character of work in advanced post-Fordism, Aureli's vision recalls the "manufactured landscapes" Canadian photographer Edward Burtinski documents in today's China: vast, panoramic views of thousands of workers employed in huge sweatshops, like ants, as far as the eye can see.[14] Aureli's scenes share with Burtinski the feeling of seduction and fear, attraction and repulsion in front of the sublime and the unrepresentable. So while it figures powerfully the scale of global capitalism's collective enslavement, banishing anything that might interfere with the unity of the production cycle and with architecture's function—as Tafuri would say—to "organize" that cycle, Aureli's proposal fails absolutely to offer any kind of utopian alternative.

This is perhaps the place to note how such a stance of "radical realism" bears a strong family resemblance to Massimo Cacciari's 1970s theorizings on "negative thought"—a nihilistic version of workerism that as Franco Fortini noted, ran the risk of embracing a cynical, technocratic vision of capitalism's advance towards an ultimate, but somehow always deferred, goal of a classless society.[15] The unfortunate effects of this stance have become all too apparent, recently, in Cacciari's politics as mayor of Venice, where he has distinguished himself by promoting the city's near-complete destruction at the hands of a mega-tourism industry, not to mention his role as a rising television personality in Berlusconi's media empire.[16]

If Aureli's work might thus be faulted for failing to explore a utopian alternative through *architectural*, as well as political means—if, in other words, his position seems to tend towards a simple reversal of the aesthetic concerns of autonomous architecture twenty years ago—how might one attempt to reformulate an idea of autonomy as a collective project in which the aesthetic *and* the political are inseparable, co-extensive dimensions of design?

It has now become a commonplace to observe how, following the crisis of the 70s, the neo-Kantian idea of autonomy espoused by Eisenman and others, which presumed to divorce architecture completely from the world of politics and economics, merely prepared the ground for its re-entry into the commodified world of the "culture industry," as Martin puts it, playing "right into the hands of the demand for maximum spectacularisation."[17] If this paradox replays, on a much lighter register to be sure, the same drama of betrayal that Benjamin described in the 1930s as the aestheticisation of politics, it may be instructive to consider some of the latter's comments, as noted in his lesser-known and as yet untranslated *Letter from Paris (1)* (1935).[18]

Paraphrasing broadly, Benjamin basically argued two points: the first is what we might call aestheticism's risk of exposure, the fact that the more one tries to sever one's links to a fallen world of politics, the stronger is the attraction, the temptation, and the material advantages of doing just the opposite.[19] I believe this is sufficiently demonstrated in the careers of many one-time proponents of autonomous architecture. Benjamin's second point was that the instrumentalisation of the art for art's sake tradition by fascism was not inevitable (Benjamin's examples here were right-wing literary figures like Filippo Tommaso Marinetti or Gottfried Benn).[20] As he noted, nothing in the history of aestheticism drew it fatally to fascist monumentalism; the same tradition might just as well have taken an opposite political direction—as it did, in fact, with constructivism and surrealism. Instead, Benjamin described the meeting of aestheticism and right-wing politics as a marriage of convenience, an "inherently contradictory juncture" that was, by its very nature, unstable and reversible. If this point opens up a margin of freedom in what many have tended to see as an incurable flaw of aestheticism, it also underscores the responsibilities of *choosing one's side* that will always come into play in any serious attempt to construct an architecture of autonomy.

To sum up, in reply to Peggy Deamer's question about the hope for radical agendas within the discourse of autonomy, it would seem that Aureli's chiasmic reversal has at least the potential to remobilize the flagging discourse of autonomy towards new and better prospects. This would mean reconfiguring the discourse of autonomy around the conditions of political subjectivity imposed by neo-liberalism—along the lines, for instance, of what Jacques Rancière describes as the essence of the political: "the part that has no part."[21]It would also mean the recovery of the lost universalist discourse of human nature and emancipation that was central to Modern Architecture, without which any notion of autonomy as a collective project is bound to remain partial.[22]

Finally, to the extent that the chiasmus I have been exploring derives much of its force from Benjamin's more basic opposition between aestheticized politics and politicized art, an architecture of autonomy would necessarily work to develop to the fullest possible extent a *politicized theory and practice of design* that is openly opposed to the dominant business model of the profession and that envisions the reversal of neo-liberalism as its most immediate political goal. At a government level, such a prospect would mean, for starters, massive public investments in housing, infrastructure, health, education, and welfare programs in an effective and complete rollback of Reaganism at a scale equal or greater than what it was able to accomplish. The size of such investments would have to be at least as great as those employed starting in 2007 to resuscitate the financial industry— short of which, as David Harvey notes, no real alternative to the neo-liberal city is possible.[23] Architecture in the broadest sense is an essential means to start this process and the challenge is to rethink the discipline from such a reversed political perspective.

Not the least value of the chiasmus as a rhetorical trope is that it makes possible to imagine such reversals, despite forty years of relentless free-market triumphalism, and to work towards them. In much the same way Debord described the spectacle as the "inverted image" of real life, and the present neo-liberal order "an adequate demonstration, in reverse, of our own project." Giorgio Agamben in very similar terms called alienation the "inverse image" of humanity's potential, which for that very reason contained within itself the promise of emancipation. To conceive the present in such antinomic terms is not to argue for a simple return to a preceding state. It merely posits the *possibility* of a political project and, therefore, also its *necessity*. The reversible logic of the chiasmus has a force of its own. It is the same one Marx alluded to when he noted, in a letter to Ruge:

> You cannot say that I hold the present time in too much esteem: and yet if I don't despair of it, its on account of its own desperate situation, which fills me with hope.[24]

14

2

Architecture, the Built
and the Idea of Socialism

David Cunningham

I want to open my comments by placing together, as if to produce a fragmentary montage of contemporary architectural problematics, three questions or statements, one from each of my interlocutors. The first is from Peggy Deamer and asks the question of whether there is still "any hope for a radical agenda within the discourse of [architectural] autonomy" as it has been "presented in the Anglo-American context"; a presentation she associates with a valorization of "architecture's divorce from politics and the economy." The second comes from Libero Andreotti, and poses the question of whether (with my emphasis) a "corporate re-engineering of design...effectively *subordinates* architecture to optimizing 'parameters' with no other ambition than to build more or less." Finally, let me place alongside these Erik Swyngedouw's last speculative question: "What, if anything, can radical planners and architects learn from the 'insurgent architects' that have animated so much of urban rebellions in recent years?"

To varying degrees, I will attempt to address each of these three propositions in what follows. However, I want to begin by posing a rather blunter question: if what is at stake in each of these propositions is how (or whether it is possible) to constitute an emancipatory project for *architecture*, then what exactly do we mean here, today, by "architecture" itself?

Now, this is, no doubt, something of a philosopher's question, rather than, say, an architectural critic's or historian's, let alone a practitioner's. Nonetheless, it is important to note that it involves far more than simply a "conceptual" or "semantic" issue, let alone an abstractly "ontological" one. Indeed, on the contrary, it engages a series of very real social and historical divisions— including those between "mental and manual labor"—through which contemporary "architecture," and the figure of the "architect," are constituted. This much is apparent in the ongoing issues of a politics of autonomy to which Peggy rightly directs us —which raise the question of what would be thought of as "proper" or "unique" to architecture *qua* architecture, such that this could be "autonomized," and hence accorded its independence or freedom (one historical meaning of "emancipation"). But it is also, I think, and perhaps most strikingly, apparent in the last of the questions that I began by citing, from Erik, where much would turn, I suggest, on how we think the meaning of "architecture" *across*, so to speak, the differentiation between what Erik terms "insurgent architects," on the one hand—a term he takes presumably from David Harvey, but which, post-2008, takes on a different resonance here—and, on the other, those "radical architects" who are invited to learn from them. Both the insurgents and the radicals are doing something called "architecture," but "architecture" does not evidently "mean" quite the same thing in each case.

I

As Manfredo Tafuri notes in his preface to the second Italian edition of *Theories and History of Architecture*, one must start first, then, by resisting at this point any "identification of particular disciplines...and of the present institutions with perennial and metahistorical 'values'."[1] If what concerns us is the possible relationship between architecture and, say, "politics," which thus invites some inquiry into the specific "nature" of each, this is immediately complicated by the fundamental *historicity* of the terms, institutions and practices at stake. Asking "what is" architecture *or* politics may be an "ontological" question, but it is only so to the degree that "ontology" can itself be thoroughly histori-cized, such as to recognize that there *is no* "essential" nature to either, and hence no unchanging relationship between them. (While my focus is on the historicity of architecture, the same should be said of both "politics" and "emancipation" of course; see, for example, Reinhart Kosselleck's typically exact "historical semantics" of the concept of emancipation in his *The Practice of Conceptual History*.[2]) This is why assessing the claim that archi-tecture today can have an emancipatory status cannot simply be, as Tafuri again remarks, in a late interview in *Casabella*, reduced to a question of addressing the "failure of modern architecture" "in itself" —as if such "failure" were simply the function of some opportunity more or less willfully squandered by individual architects or movements themselves. (Whatever a "partisan, militant Left historiography of modernism" might "look like" — to cite one of Libero's initial questions—it would certainly have to start from somewhere other than this.) Rather, it is a question of a lucid and sober accounting for "what architects could do when certain things weren't possible and when they were."[3] This is, of course, also another way of phrasing my own question: what would be involved, today, in identifying those "tasks which capitalist development has taken away from architecture," as well as of what Libero describes as the *subordination* of archi-tecture to other institutions or practices that this may entail.

To take a single example, consider what then, in the short book *Façade* overseen by Alejandro Zaera-Polo and produced as part of Koolhaas's "Elements of Architecture" series for the 2014 Venice Biennale, is referred to as the contemporary "rise of 'facadism,' the focus on the façade to the detriment of the rest", in which, "rather than a coordination of the elements that make up the whole, the façade is now a thing in and of itself, in the form of a skin and a shape."[4] While Zaera-Polo himself has often apparently celebrated this as a kind of liberation (or autonomy?) of architecture *qua* architecture, its corollary is also what can, I think, only be regarded as a "realist" surrendering of the other traditional dimensions of building production (program, organization, and so on) to developers, engineers or various other "consultants"; a "surrendering" that would seem to accompany a simultaneous shrinking, at an urban level, of the "architect's role" to "a form of city-branding, addressing the packaging of buildings and cities rather than their (social) content."[5]

It is easy (and not exactly wrong) to respond to this, and to the reduction of architecture to spectacle that it can seem to legitimate, with what would thus be a series of both aesthetic and ethico-political criticisms of the kind that Hal Foster, for example, mobilizes so effectively in the case of Gehry.[6] (Although there is also the danger here that political critique can quickly drift into simple *moralism*, automatically equating the attention to "surface" with the "superficial," and thereby dealing with it as if it constituted something like a predominantly *ethical* failing on the part of individual architects. Lefebvre's explicit critique of a leftist "asceticism" in the recently discovered *Architecture of Enjoyment*, and of the suspicion of sensuousness and consumption that often underlies an anxiety about shifting class boundaries, is no doubt relevant in this respect.) Yet, just as historically significant might be the fact that, as Zaera-Polo also acknowledges, even here, where its specialization might seem most secure, if the "façade is one of the few remaining elements that has not been forgotten by architects," it is also the case that "most now lack the competence to design the increasingly complex details demanded by contemporary facades. Fabrication and mounting are increasingly farmed out to specialized consultants…" One does not have to follow the implicit judgements— artistic, philosophical or political—that accompany it (and I don't) to agree with the general thrust of Zaera-Polo's observation that the "agency of architecture" no longer remains simply with "the authorial architect imposing a will-to-form," and to wonder what this means for our understanding of "architecture" itself.

As he continues: "Decisions involve a growing field of agents, each with differing perspectives...For example, the role that companies like Dow Chemical, DuPont or Rockwool play in the construction of the material environments today is enormous and unprecedented in the history of architecture, but they have not been recognized yet in terms of their agency and cultural significance."[7]

One "basic banality" *of* architectural historiography—to borrow Libero's felicitous phrase—might then be the simple reminder that the concepts of architecture and, crucially, of "the architect", as we understand those terms today, and the kinds of limits or boundaries that they draw—concepts that, among other things, generate the necessity for the quote marks that Erik places around "insurgent architects"—are no more than five centuries old at most, and by no means unchanging. Indeed, it is perhaps *only* with the emergence of capitalist modernity that the "architect" appears as such, in an institutional, professional or disciplinary sense; a sense stabilized around the late eighteenth century. (In many countries, its professional sense is also, of course, a *legal* sense, guaranteed by the state, which thereby gives a monopoly over certain forms of building construction.) In this way, architecture's modern construction as more than *just* a matter of building production—which lies at the root of Peggy's observation that architecture's "being design" has come to identify it with a form of what Lazzarato and others call "immaterial labor"—is also its necessary formation as an "independent" set of structures and discourses, internally and externally related to the totality of such structures within modern society as a whole, from education to law to art to political economy proper. Among other things, this is why a query (perhaps implicit in Peggy's question) as to whether architectural emancipation—both an emancipation of "itself" from its own institutional limits and its potential contribution to some wider social emancipation—requires breaking down a division of labor between, for example, forms of "mental" and "manual" labor, and the hierarchies attendant upon this, is also a question about the *definition* (and possible re-definition) of architecture as such, since, long before anyone ever thought of "immaterial labor" — and whether it is articulated in the name of "art" or, say, technical expertise — this very division *just is* the basis of the modern constitution of "architecture."[8]

A critical reflection upon the "emancipatory" potentials of architecture thus has to incorporate an historical account of architecture's specifically modern status *as an institution*, a status which opens up an irreducible non-identity with regard to the actual material practices to which it relates, and that cannot merely be voluntaristically willed away, since it is embedded in economic, technological and legal structures that are not themselves "architectural." This is, I take it, Tafuri's consistent point in framing his own historiographical work, from the 1968 *Theories and History* onwards. It is however less about a "fatalistic" *Realpolitik* concerning the socio-political potency of current architectural possibility (to re-deploy Libero's terms) than it is about our need for a more developed account of the evolving sets of institutional and ideological "meanings" that have historically generated and reproduced the modern idea of the "architectural" itself; not least because any productive "partisan, militant Left historiography" of modern architecture would have to interrogate exactly *what* and *where* the borders defining its "object of study" might be.

In fact, the question of how to think such borders of the architectural has been central to much of the historiography of architectural modernity from its very beginnings — a point exemplified by the work of Siegfried Giedeon, who writes in *Building in France, Building in Iron, Building in Ferro-Concrete* that: "ARCHITECTURE NO LONGER HAS ANY RIGID BOUNDARIES."[9] (Giedeon is thinking here of the effects of the new openness of actual built structure, for which the Eiffel Tower was, for him, one crucial reference point, as well as of the collapse of a clear distinction between architectural and urban space, but, as the latter in particular suggests, such lack of "rigid boundaries" relates, too, to the very *definition* of architecture vis-à-vis built structure in general.) Any "partisan, militant Left historiography" today needs to recover something of this dynamic of questioning also. So, just as, for instance, one of the achievements of modern(ist) historiography was to "read" Albert Kahn's factory constructions for Ford *as architecture*, in the face of Kahn's own distinction between what he called the *"art* of architecture" and the *"business* of building"—a "reading" that precisely made Kahn a pivotal figure for the Modern Movement—so we would need to think about what the contemporary equivalents to such distinctions between architecture and mere "building" might be, and what would be at stake in complicating or challenging this today. What would it mean, for example, to write an "anonymous history" of the twenty-first-century built environment, as Giedeon described the project of his own 1948 book *Mechanization Takes Command*? If nothing else, there would certainly be something to be said for the necessary orientation away from the fixation on architectural "authorship" common to both academic and journalistic architectural criticism that this would involve. As the novelist Adam Hollinghurst writes in his review of the 2004 *Phaidon Atlas of Contemporary World Architecture*: "A real atlas of what is being built in the world today would be a confounding thing—a *Domesday Book* of cheapness, pretension and making do."[10] But perhaps it's precisely this kind of "real atlas," with its mapping of what Koolhaas famously terms the "junkspace" of modernity, that is needed more than ever in the face of a globalizing capitalism's ongoing production of space?

II

For me, the possibility of a "real atlas of what is being built in the world today" is a rather compelling idea. All the same, its corresponding *danger* is that it invites a "merely theoretical" reconciliation between "architecture" and "building" *tout court*. The tendency to expand a definition of architecture to more or less everything "spatial" or "social" in its entirety is, at any rate, a longstanding temptation among architects and theorists—a temptation that might well be understood as a means of countering architecture's effective historical *subordination* (to use Libero's term) to urbanism or 'total design' via a re-definition of the latter as always already the property of architecture itself; what Jonathan Hill terms a characteristically "protectionist measure."[11]This has a long history, going back at least to the early twentieth century, and is exemplified in someone like Gropius's distinctively modern notion of a "total architecture," in which the architect would give "form" at every scale. Today, encouraged by a heady brew of post-Deleuzian immanence, Latourian flat ontology and cybernetics, it finds one contemporary manifestation in, for example, the various resurgent naturalisms definitive of much "cutting-edge" architectural practice, for which, according to the current director of the Architectural Association, Brett Steele, "what is called architecture is barely distinguishable from the behaviors making up the natural world all around it—a world, that is, where bodies, organisms, systems and even disciplines share one thing above all else in common: their own malleability."[12]

In his recent introduction to *Towards an Architecture of Enjoyment*, Lukasz Stanek sets out rather well some of the dilemmas all of this entails. As he puts it: since space is actually "produced by many agents, architects arguably among the least influential," architecture must seemingly *either* find itself reduced to narrow disciplinary protectionism, with the risk that it simply confirms its own "sublime uselessness," in Tafuri's evocative formulation—"an utter alienation mistaken for independence"[13]—*or* seek to claim a wider remit, with the consequence that architects find themselves "held responsible for something they cannot control";[14] a fate that is very evident in those accounts that condemn something vaguely defined as "modernism" for all the failings of mass housing and spatial planning since the second world war.[15]

In his one essay devoted to modern architecture, Adorno notes that architectural work "is conditioned by a social antagonism over which the greatest architecture has no power: the same society which developed human productive energies to unimaginable proportions has chained them to conditions of production imposed upon them"[16]—perhaps as good a "truism" as any to place at the heart of architectural discourses of the Left today. But it does so in a fashion that *both* articulates what would seem the minimal criteria of any project of "emancipation"—that it seek, in conformity with the historical semantics of the term "emancipation" itself, to *unchain* certain possibilities from those current "conditions of production imposed upon them"—*and*, at the same time, articulates the profound limits placed upon even the "greatest architecture" as the vehicle through which any such project might be seriously furthered today.

If this means, as a "basic banality," that to ask fundamental questions about what "might help reconstitute a genuine architecture of the Left today" (Libero) *cannot but be* then, first of all, a question about architecture's relation to capitalism, it is partly for this reason that discussions surrounding autonomy in architectural theory—to return to one of Peggy's questions—often seem to me misguided simply because they imagine that "autonomy" is something that one might be straightforwardly for or against, endorse or refuse, rather than, first and foremost, a contradictory *reality* in which all architecture *necessarily* finds itself enmeshed. Indeed, it is, above all, the "failure" to recognize this reality itself that is, I think, for Tafuri, "ideological"; the intrinsic failure of architecture *qua* architecture to reflect upon the social conditions of its own institutional status, and the divisions of labor sustaining it. Architecture's incapacity to operate critically can then be read as a problem inherent within the narrowness of a critical *architecture*—as opposed to a critique *of* architecture—as such. As he famously puts it (and the point still stands): "To search for an alternative within the structures that condition the very character of architectural design is indeed an obvious contradiction in terms."[17] From the perspective of an emancipatory project, the problems within which architecture finds itself enmeshed are simply not themselves architectural, but the problems of an "unfree society" (Adorno).

In this sense, the problem of "autonomy" is best understood as the basis for an historical analysis of architecture's unfolding *social* determination in capitalist modernity, its production out of historically specific social relations. If this means that all autonomy must be, at some level, an illusion—since it is, as Adorno puts it, simultaneously *both* autonomous *and* "social fact"—it is at the same time, paradoxically, all-too real, insofar as the social separation it marks determines architecture's (from one perspective, increasingly narrow) place within the divided reality of capitalist modernity as a whole; a separation which architecture *qua* architecture itself cannot simply overcome. A "radical" architecture might "like to break out of this entanglement," "yet, it can only rattle its chains in vain as long as it remains trapped in an entangled society."[18]

If this then certainly demands a certain "courageous act of conscious realism" (as Tafuri terms it) on the part of the contemporary Left, it should not thereby be reducible to any simple "fatalism," or *Realpolitik*, of the type against which Libero rightly cautions. The opposition between "fatalism" and "voluntarism" is—like that between reform and revolution (to which it always seems, more or less obscurely, to be related)—one very familiar to the history of the Left. But it may not be the most productive here. (To paraphrase *The 18th Brumaire of Louis Bonaparte*, this would be another "truism" to add to the list: humanity makes its own history, but not under conditions of its own choosing!) At any rate, if one certainly needs to be alive to the risks of turning "reality" itself into an ideology, which can indeed easily appear the case in "the so-called New Pragmatism" (and which also seems, I think, to lie behind Peggy's question as to whether "the discourse of globalization [has] harmed, usurped or displaced architecture theory's critical agenda" because of the ways in which it can seem to reinforce capitalism's "inevitability"), then, equally, I'm not sure that we can do without some measure of "disenchanted" confrontation with the realities of the conditions and relations of production in which architecture must operate if we're to get anywhere in thinking about its possibilities and limits today.

From this perspective, one (in some ways) unfortunate corollary of recent architectural criticism and theory's under-standable focus on "the use of star designers in massive specu-lative building campaigns," as Libero describes it, *even where this has been approached critically*, is that—despite the so-called "crisis of the object" often said to be definitive of modern architecture in general—it has resulted in a renewed focus upon the individual "work." There are important reasons for this, and, in fact, insofar as the reduction of architecture *to* such singular objects is part of what seems to reinforce its contemporary "political" impotence—to the degree that its radicalism becomes simply a "formal" license to construct novel skins and facades for art galleries and the odd "signature" office building, while the rest of the built environment is "outsourced" to other kinds of building professional—it tends to *confirm* the "crisis of the object," in Tafuri's sense, rather than refute it; up to a point at least (although, as I have argued elsewhere, it also underesti-mates the functionalization *of* this return to the "aesthetic" object that renders it paradoxically "useful" to processes of commodifi-cation, as in so-called "urban branding"[19]). However, at the same time—and this takes me back to Hollinghurst's hypothetical "real atlas of what is being built in the world today"—one short-coming of recent architectural criticism and history (critical or otherwise) is that it often gives us, as a result, little overall sense of what is actually being built, or the forms and conditions of production under which this takes place. This involves, for example, *both*, on the one hand, what Patrick Keiller identifies as "the new landscapes which have evolved as a result of computer-driven change," which are often "peripheral" to urban centers, and "either ephemeral and relatively insubstantial" (and, hence, effectively "unseen")—the logistics warehouse, the container port, the business park[20]—*and*, on the other, the massive "informal" settlements or "shantytowns" that constitute much of the rapidly growing urban world of the global South. The involvement of anyone bearing the title "architect" in *both* is, of course, usually minimal if not non-existent. A first question then might be what is at stake in considering—if it is possible or desirable to do so—such building *as* "architecture"; something that would clearly require, at the very least, a huge rethinking of what Tafuri calls "the paraphernalia of the traditional categories of judgment."[21] (One would not be entirely wrong, of course, to wonder whether, in the end, Tafuri ever really undertakes such a profound rethinking himself.) This would not exactly break down existing divisions of labor—something that would, *in reality*, require a far more wholesale transformation of the conditions and relations of production; or, in other words, social revolution—but it would at least interrogate, with due "realism," the very real divisions under which the non-identity of architecture with building production operates today. This would, then, allow us, for example, not only to think more clearly about what it means to re-conceive architecture (or, more specifically, architectural design) as a form of "immaterial labor," as Peggy suggests, but also to think seriously—alongside the straightforward ethical condemnation that it has rightly received—about the realities that lie behind, say, Zaha Hadid's now-notorious comments concerning migrant workers in Qatar. To quote: "I have nothing to do with the workers. I think that's an issue the government—if there's a problem—should pick up."[22] It is because of this that it does indeed seem legitimate to think of architecture as something of a privileged site for understanding the changing character of "intellectual labor" in capitalist development more generally, if not necessarily for actually transforming it in the progressive ways that "we" might like.

III

Attempts to identify socialist or communist forms developing immanently to capitalism itself—that "real movement which abolishes the present state of things"—are (not least in the name of a certain "realism") understandably thin on the ground these days. Nonetheless, I continue to think that any project of emancipation, in architecture as elsewhere, remains fundamentally dependent upon this—one that, if it entails its own "courageous act of conscious realism," might involve, above all, a need to re-think architecture's relationship to wider issues of *planning*, and, through this, to the state, today. I have written about this at some length elsewhere, so I won't belabor the point too much here.[23] But it is, at any rate, against this backdrop that it is worth reflecting a little upon contemporary architecture's inheritance—on the other side, so to speak, of the neo-liberal "counter-revolution" of the last few decades—of those "emancipatory discourses" that were once tied to the emergence, politics and actualities of various social-democratic projects, in Europe especially, as well as, of course, to post-colonial nation-state building in the mid twentieth century.

Now, there can be little doubt that the actual histories of these discourses did indeed tend, ultimately, to limit such "emancipation" to the politics of modernizing capitalist social relations, as Tafuri and Tronti both, in their different ways, suggest. (It remains a more open question as to what degree the forms of architectural production carried out under so-called "really existing socialism," and the projects of nation-state building that they supported in other parts of the world, can or cannot be incorporated into this analysis; the reductive analysis of the Soviet Union as nothing more than a "state capitalism," common to many council communists and Trotskyites, has, at any rate, never seemed to me terribly convincing, and tends to underplay what, however problematically or abhorrently, was indeed "socialist" in the former Eastern Europe and elsewhere.) However, if it would thus be hard to disagree with an assertion that, today, "architectural emancipation" would require going beyond such social-democratic, socialist or "Fordist" parameters, so as to reclaim some broader, renewed horizon of future social transformation, we need to be equally careful not to imagine, as is sometimes supposed, that this also effaces the need to continue to think about the question of architecture's relation to something like the state as a kind of *necessary* mediator of social collectivity—without which we risk the delusion that *any* modern society could do with forms of mediation, representation or abstraction—and to changing state forms today.

From the perspective of a "partisan, militant historiography," the history of modern architecture certainly still has much to tell us about both the possibilities *and* limitations of different forms of would-be emancipatory politics in this respect—concerning, for example, the histories of urban infrastructural planning or mass housing—as regards architecture's potential role (however limited) in struggles for new "rights" to the city. (It is here, too, that, for example, both Tafuri's analysis of the limitations of inter-war social democratic urbanism and Red Vienna, and Tronti's contrary account of the latter as what Aureli calls a "realistic" attempt to deal with the objective conditions of capitalism, and to build some stable form of resistance to them, still have much to teach us.[24]) At any rate, a justified suspicion that "reformist" or "social-democratic" projects are restricted, ultimately, to the management or planning *of* capitalist development itself, as well as to the amelioration of class struggle, shouldn't occlude the role that these might play when viewed from the long-term horizon of some more *systematic* "social transformation."

This is partly an issue of temporality regarding what we might mean by social "revolution" itself. As Domenico Losurdo rightly argues, today perhaps more than ever, we need to recover a "formulation made by the later Marx, according to whom the intensification of the contradiction between productive forces and relations of production leads not to a single revolution, but rather to 'an epoch of social revolution'."[25] (It is here too, no doubt, that the Gramscian model of building hegemony remains both attractive and useful in a number of respects, along with some rather broader Marxian discussions of "transition.") At the very least, it seems important to me, for this reason, to complicate considerably a tendency—broadly common to, say, Badiou, Rancière and Hardt and Negri—to reduce the State *tout court* (as if it were simply one "thing") to the role of "capital's executives," and, hence, not only social democracy, but socialism as such to the limits of a management of capitalism.[26]

As against this, the danger in broadly dismissing, even denigrating, the twentieth century histories of "social-democratic projects" and welfarism—and the attraction to fantasies of the type expressed by Negri, that the "end of the welfare state leaves a large space in the social autonomy of the multitude for the reconstruction of the common"[27]—is that, too often, would-be radical calls to self-organization and creativity, understood as one legacy of the critiques of "modernist" planning of the 1950s and '60s, run the risk of simply mirroring, today, those ideologies of self-organization and creativity attributed to the neo-liberal market as such, and, at worse, can serve to perform such ideologies work for them. (While, in fact, misrecognising the degree to which neo-liberalism does not in fact "negate" forms of planning to anything like the extent that its rhetoric suggests. What else, after all, is "logistics"? Urban infrastructure, services, planning, building, etc are, as often as not, not so much "liberated" today to the purportedly self-organizing capacities of the market, as simply contracted out to private companies who are given effective monopoly rights over whatever the State previously managed.[28]) More generally, I frequently have a sense that contemporary leftist politics, in architecture as elsewhere, can feel constrained by a political horizon still defined by May '68, and by struggles against social democratic reformism and Stalinist parties that are hardly our own.[29] This was, at any rate, part of the gist of my own question concerning the merits of Boltanski and Chiapello's work that seeks to trace the recuperation of earlier leftist and counter-cultural demands for "emancipation" within contemporary neoliberal politics and managerialism.[30]

At least part of what might thus be needed is a way to re-energize a Left emancipatory architectural or urban planning project's association *with the Modern*, rather than, as many contemporary "ultra-leftists" seem to wish to do, to escape from it. (This is something, I take it, that current European debates around so-called "accelerationism" are at least attempting to engage, albeit in rather theoretically flimsy ways.[31]) Such would, in turn, require more complex historiographies of the "successes" and "failures" of those past "modernities" posited by social-democratic urban projects now gone, and of the strategic engagement *with* state institutions, at various levels, that these involved. But this may require us to complicate, too, some hardenings of the reform versus revolution opposition with which the Left has, at times, become rather too comfortable, if only because, as Jameson observes, social democracy's "inevitable failure constitutes the basic lesson, the fundamental pedagogy, of a genuine Left": "The Welfare State was an achievement; its internal contradictions are those of capitalism and not a failure of social and collective concern."[32] The ways in which "radical architecture" (often not institutionally recognized as such) in various Latin American countries—on which Justin

McGuirk's recent book *Radical Cities* offers an excellent primer—has constructed a certain agency by both working with and through state institutions, and at times resisting them, in the effort to build mass housing and infrastructure in some of the most impoverished urban areas of the continent, provides both some inspiration and a kind of test case here for what McGuirk terms "the power to convey a political will at the service of the people, to communicate modernization and the right to housing."[33]

This is not to say, as a consequence, that there is nothing to learn from, say, the necessarily more "ephemeral" practices of "insurgent architects," if I understand what Erik is getting at by this phrase correctly. Far from it. But I'm wary of some more expansive valorization of this to the degree that problems of social revolution can, in an "ultra-leftist" contempt for any suspicion of reformism or pragmatism, easily slip into a simple valorization of "revolt" (to employ yet another classic Marxian opposition) as an end in itself—something which seems especially fatal for any attempt to re-think a possible politics of "architecture" beyond its own current limits today. The tendency in much recent architectural and urban theory to think, for example, that any seemingly "unprogramed" space is axiomatically "radical"—as against the "discipline" of planning—signifies, it seems to me, little more than the current crisis of Left ideas of revolution themselves; a now-familiar tactic of turning defeat into spurious victory. One consequence is that, as I have argued elsewhere, a collective historical temporality of *systemic* transformation and liberation is displaced by an increasingly apocalyptic celebration of interruption or dissensus, a faith in disruptive "singular and precarious acts" of democracy, or a metaphysics of the "event."[34] The price paid is the loss of any idea of a *social* (rather than just "political") revolution, the duration of which would be measured in decades, if not, indeed, centuries. David Harvey's point that one should be "careful not to demolish ... too readily" the collective (if "alienated") structures that capitalism has produced to "feed the world" (and to house it) remains important in this regard.[35]

Thinking seriously and soberly about what this might involve for processes of systematic social transformation, and of the role that differing conceptions of the "architectural" might play within it, entails a re-engagement with some old questions about "appropriation" or what Brecht called "re-functioning" (*Umfunktionierung*). But it also means holding to the idea that, as Immanuel Wallerstein once wrote, there is little "interest in a 'socialism' that claims to be a 'temporary' moment of transition towards Utopia. There is interest only in a concretely historical socialism, one that meets the maximum defining characteristics of a historical system that maximizes equality and equity, one that increases humanity's control over its own life (democracy), and liberates the imagination."[36]

3

Architects, Really

Peggy Deamer

I

In the question put forward by my fellow authors, I was struck by the fact that the term "architect" is only used twice. "Architecture," from me as well, revealed itself to be the object of investigation. At first I only paid attention to the distinction in the questions between those that, in the search for the locus of emancipatory work, emphasized the theorists and those that emphasized practice; between those that want to correct theories' failures to emancipate us and those that want to blame and change practice. In both cases, the implicit fault was an inability to persuade. But who is the subject of persuasion? "Architecture" struck me as a non-specific audience. Aren't we trying to convince "architects" that they can/should operate differently?

I shudder a bit to come down on the side of addressing the "architect"—so practical! so past rehabilitation! It is a bit like insisting on a strict definition of "architecture" to include only the buildings, not the images or discourses that surround them. But if we agree that persuasion is our task, a more focused analysis of the audience is strategic. That persuasion itself might be a dirty occupation for neo-Marxists—identified with rhetorical insincerity and capitalist ideology—is worth considering...but only for one moment. It is not just my belief that we all need to get our hands dirty (meaning, leaving behind the high ground of pure theory) but also David Harvey's moving text, "The Insurgent Architect at Work" [1] (thank you Erik Swyngedouw) in which his military-like seven "theatres" of operation gives strategies to 'the architect" (and not merely "architecture") "to persuade people to look beyond the borders of that myopic world of daily life."

An architect and teacher like me is hyper-aware of what is cool for the next generation of architects; for better or worse, I feel obliged to (and have come to feel secure in) couching my advice in cool contexts. If much of what I want to talk about relates to professional practice (not cool) or to Marxist theory (not cool), I can appeal to entrepreneurialism (very cool) and expanded notions of creativity in the digital age (pretty cool). This might seem sad, untruthful, or worse, but here we are. But alas, we are fighting; this is a fight. We need to know our point of attack. We (theorists) need to construct the desire for change; we need to persuade.

I want to clarify what issues are at stake here for me when we focus our attention on the architect. The first is to identify the architect as a worker. (How fortuitous it is that Harvey does not only reference "architects" but "at work" as well!) It is my belief that architects don't believe that they do work; they design, they make contributions to the built environment, they follow a calling, but they don't work/labor and they don't (think they) operate in the nexus of supply and demand, labor and materials. Not only does theory have a huge role to play in addressing our labor-aphasia, but also it must convince architects that we are not "other" to the society of users, owners, developers we serve; we don't merely hand over our gifts of a better world to these people, we operate in that world, one that unites us by work. Until we identify as workers, we can't identify with other workers—the rest of the world. Part of our theoretical work then is to persuade architects that "designing" rather than "following a calling" is a job and as such is not pathetic, dull, or unimaginative but socially grounded.

The second issue in our "architecture" cause is concentrating not on the products that architects produce—buildings, cities— but on the process by which we produce them. With fair labor?

With gender equality? With respect for clients and users? With healthy respect and distain for the technology we employ? Too often the social viability of the architect is measured by the efficacy of the product—good or bad building? Good or bad city?—and not by the social viability of the organizations—internal or external to the office—that produced it. As Ed Ford in his *The Details of Modern Architecture* (and repeated by me many times) has pointed out, in so far as the nineteenth century had social concerns, it was for the workers/producers constructing the buildings; in so far as the twentieth century had social concerns, it was for the users/consumers using the buildings—this of course reflecting the shift in interest in social economics in the early twentieth century from production to consumption.[2] Not only does the void need to be addressed, the architect/worker needs to enter our contemporary social consciousness as well. S/he was left out in the nineteenth century because s/he was assumed to be a member of the petty bourgeoisie and in the twentieth century because s/he was a producer, not a consumer. This is my resistance to discourses (including much of David Harvey's work) that assume that the singular realm of "the social" is the city. Yes, but it is also in our very own architectural house. I believe it is impossible for us architects to imagine the ideal social realm when we operate naively in the context of abusive, illegal, and undemocratic work.

The third issue at stake in focusing our persuasive tactics on "architects," not "architecture," is agency. Yes, capitalism and globalism move the spheres of power in ways that elude agency while also constructing it. But architects can be agents of change; they can construct new arenas of production and new desires for emancipation. Here, Harvey's "The Insurgent Architect at Work" is consistently illuminating, even as he clearly envisions a metaphorical "architect" that is more citizen than trained architect. Insisting that the political resides wholly in the personal—"The moment of universality is not a final moment of revelation or absolute truth. I construe it...as a moment of existential decisions, a moment of "either/or" praxis, when certain principles are materialized through action in the world."—he reminds us theorists that our work is to persuade architects to such "moments of universality" and that one by one, these architects in turn act as agents of change.

But who are these architects if we want to be more specific than Harvey's general citizen? On the one hand, they are certainly more than registered architects; the class we are referring to is made up of anyone deploying architectural knowledge: students, teachers, critics, designers, landscape architects, urban designers, planners. Indeed, as we shall argue further on, the class could include the engineers, the fabricators and constructors of our buildings, neighborhoods and cities. On the other, they are subjects that are more than their work; the "architectural worker" is, as Marx reminds us, a human subject through and through, for whom architecture sets up certain social relations but not all; whose pleasure or displeasure of work invades the rest of his/her humanity, but whose humanity is not only defined by this work. Thus, any discussion about the work of an architect is not limited to the hours "at work" but to a person's general subjectivity as performed in this career.

II

With this "architect"-focused interrogation, we can turn to four reformulated questions posed by my fellow authors (and me) that I believe are the most pressing: A) What is the nature— material or immaterial—of architectural work and with it the architectural worker? B) How does "the contemporary context"— digital, open-sourced, project driven, social-media shaped, neo-liberal—shape an emancipatory project? C) Is there or what is the role of utopianism in our capitalist context? And D) Who controls the architectural agenda?

A. What is the nature—material or immaterial—of architectural work and with it the architectural worker?

As architectural workers we produce drawings and designs that lead to a physical object. Our objects are material but our work is not. The distinction is important but generally under-examined and destructively interpreted, which is to say, the discipline of architecture has taken the worst of both models. From material labor, we take a Taylorist model of production, with a factory line movement from concept, to design development, to working drawings, to construction oversight...to those, in other words, who, apparently seamlessly, continue that chain: from contractor to sub-contractors to fabricators (and the increased assumption of down graded workers, from principal to staff to blue-collar workers). We then overlay on this a corporate model of management—a principal/manager-to-staff organizational hierarchy in which the staff are subject to the demands of the project architect's whims and timetable. But unlike these material labor models, architectural workers have no bargaining power, no unions, no control of schedule, no recourse upon being fired, no paid overtime. All of the *undesirable* aspect of immateriality—precarity, long working hours, casuality, tolerance of inequality—dominate. In this, the touted advantages of immaterial work—creativity, caring, respect for women's work, self-realization, autonomy—are smothered by the office structure that allows neither independence nor control over the content or form of work. Creativity here is governed by uncertainty, itself not bad (it is a precondition of self-realization and innovation) but without management techniques in place to negotiate its negative effects. Psychic damage associated with immaterial labor follows: self-exploitation, the side effect of immaterial labor when one over-identifies with work, is not even justified by the reward of authorship bragging rights.

The culprit in this distorted confluence of two types of labor is the obsession with object-making—object-making allowing the image of material production. We get paid by the object (percentage of construction, flat-fee, hourly payment with a percentage of construction cap), we get published by the object, we are motivated by the object, we staff up and organize our offices around the clients' objects. Being paid by the object is not just a conceptual problem (it is piecework), it is a financial one. We are horribly paid.[3] Moreover, the object fixation precludes being rewarded for our ability to translate social readings into the buildings we produce. Being published by the object allows the public to think that we are motivated only by aesthetics and the fame that comes with formal virtuosity, not the enormous amount of research, analysis, and experience that lies behind our formal choices. Getting known for our objects works for a minority of the profession, the stars, but saddles the majority of its workers with the reputation of aesthetic and financial extravagance and social disinterest. The fact that we are published by the object, in turn, leads us to be sadly motivated by its production. This is why we don't think long term about goals, social or otherwise. Our main motivation is to get the next object and not ask the question of why we are bothering, beyond the ability to either have a photograph taken or to pay the staff. As Paolo Tombesi has pointed out, this not only ties the architect's work to the resolution of material challenges (rather than, say, spatial, social or cultural ones); it also inevitably discounts (at least economically) the conceptual side of architectural practice. This in turn restricts our interest in the proper management of the office staff. We rarely know how to organize them and the intelligence that comes with them beyond who is available for the next one-off job. Every project is seen as requiring its own taskforce for which we hire up when we get a new one or fire down when none other appears. It is not just that limitless availability of willing creative workers means staff will not protest; it is also that we fail to think and hence manage for long term ambitions.

If, in lieu of this, we indulged the best aspects of our immaterial labor's association with material labor—the fact that we direct aspects of a material worker's performance—much is to be gained. Not only can we experience and indulge that side of our work that is creative, unmeasurable, un-routine, socially-motivated and appreciative of new skills, but, if we refused to indulge the supposed privileges that come with our profession-alization—seeing instead the intricacy of our dependence on the creative knowledge that constructors bring to the design/build process—a legal and spiritual empathy would replace mutual distrust and disrespect. Bringing disciplinary autonomy into contact with construction is critical in raising the hope that archi-tectural workers have enough resources to perform in a socially viable ways.[4]

The implicit class prejudice that architects, as white collar-workers, have against blue collar workers is essential to acknowledge and transcend. This does not mean not doing away with "class" as an issue, but, redefining it and our location in it. As Harvey has indicated, the insurgent architect must work in networks, of which class is central. In his *Classes*,[5] Erik Olin Wright also indicates how class consciousness is central to a new socialism, and should be understood as part of a larger dimension of subjectivity, with three dimensions: 1. perceptions of alternatives (what legitimation was in old Marxism) 2. theories of consequences (what was mystification). 3. preferences (what was hegemony. Architects can take pleasure in complicating, if not undoing, a distinction between material and immaterial labor that was handed to us by capitalist management techniques [6] at the same time, we identify not as white or blue, but as "precarious" locating an identity with non-professional workers who fight the good fight and take risks for doing so.

B. How does "the contemporary context"—digital, open-sourced, project driven, social-media shaped, neo-liberal—shape an emancipatory project?

If the issue for architectural labor is the correct management of the materially connected immaterial nature of our work, then the contemporary condition of work puts special pressure on this type. The contemporary conditions—flexibility, autonomy, entrepreneurialism—are those handed us by neo-liberalism, and it exploits all the conditions associated with immateriality.

Harvey has pointed out that the neo-liberal agenda "can best be advanced by liberating individual entrepreneurial freedoms and skills within an institutional framework characterized by strong private property rights, free markets, and free trade."[7] Call this marketization (the process by which the market exchange increasingly comes to permeate media and cultural sectors[8]), the knowledge economy, the creative economy, or the information society—its legitimation is that culture is "the main growth areas of national and international economies, and therefore the basis of future or present prosperity."[9] Forms of creativity and knowledge which were not previously conceived as ownable are brought into the intellectual property system, making them available for the investment of capital and the making of profit, and helping to avoid the perennial problems of over-accumulation which haunt capitalism.

In the negative column for architecture, the push for commercial imperatives, especially strong in the neo-liberal context, requires any move toward a more social, emancipatory context to demonstrate its financial pay-off. The quick changes that the current economy produces increases the precariousness that is already the nature of our field. The naïveté of the Italian autonomists' optimism about immaterial and affective labor (that they are beyond and thereby undermine economics metrics; that they are the basis, with their caring and immanent cooperation, of elementary communism); of Richard Florida's "The Creative Class" (which glorifies the creative class as bourgeois gentrifiers); and of the technological determinists' (celebrating social media's breakdown of the division between production and consumption when consumers become producers and distributors, "produsage", which gleefully ignores the issue of employment and with it the alienation of labor in production)—these have all soured us architects to any optimism that might result from thinking of ourselves as creative laborers; the realities of neo-liberalism's invasion into our cultural/creative sphere described above are just too clear.

In the positive column for architecture, the "creativity" discourse has brought back a labor focus that makes this issue "cool". How do we work vis-à-vis Apple employees; care-givers? flexi-workers? freelancers? How are we financed compared to film-makers, musicians, journalists? broadcasters? How does our work get recognized and turned into cultural and economic power in comparison to clothing designers? chefs? While the "produsage" optimism ignores the real employment issues, it focuses our attention on the possibility of models of work that shift away from object-making and standard office constructs. The entire debate between material and immaterial labor articulated above would not be possible if neo-liberalism hadn't forced us to consider the source and structure of cultural—and with it, architectural—production.

Likewise, the new models of work have at their center a DIY mentality that, while consistent with neo-liberalism's cooption of the individual, has brought with it alternative processes for architectural thinking that, while self-empowering, also demands sharing and cooperation. If the autonomists were overly optimistic in this heralding socialism, they were not wrong in its cooperative characterization. With the help of advanced software technology, younger professionals are able to access knowledge and form ad-hoc teams of experts allowing them to produce quicker. Small firms can act like big firms. Precariousness is increased but the flexibility that is its reward becomes less strange and more imaginable, risky but with identifiable rewards. The old model of star architects/firm principals handing down menial tasks to willing sub-undergrundies fades away as a new generation learns that their training in media, software, and social confluence puts them at an advantage. With this comes the renewed interest in utopianism.

This balance-sheet indicates not a hedging of theoretical positioning but, rather, defines the territory that architectural work must negotiate. The multiplicity of forms that capitalism has been forced to assume because of technology and the vagaries it has brought to both production and consumption indicates not only capitalism's flexibility but its desperation. No, the revolution may not come, but we can make it dance harder, faster and in greater panic.

The key here is the management of technology and the data it accumulates to empower both the commons and the individual. This means resisting all forms of censorship; managing copyright laws for creatives' own advantage; taking proprietary software and forcing it to bend to our needs; owning our intellectual property;[10] For architects in particular, it means new forms of contracts between owners, builders, engineers, and fabricators; it means new forms of managing risk and identifying rewards.

C. Can our architectural agenda be utopian given our embeddedness in capitalism?

Harvey, in his "The Insurgent Architect at Work," is very articulate about the dialectic process of thinking the possible—trying it on—and accepting the changes to self and life that this then engenders. To think the utopian, however, is not the same as expecting utopia (or the revolution) or assuming that anything less than utopia (socialism) is a compromise or failure. To "think" utopia means not only imagining it as a place, but as a mechanism to manage work. Here, one comes to those utopians of the past that in every case put labor front and center of their various social constructs. Whether labor hours, while made more humane, were seen as something to shorten so that the good life could be experienced (Thomas More, Edward Bellamy Bellamy,

Robert Owen) or whether labor hours were seen as inherently enlightening and pleasurable (Tomasso Campanella, Charles Fourier, William Morris, Frank Lloyd Wright) the utopians knew that the creation of a good workplace was the necessary if not sufficient basis for socialism. As Adam Smith, Foucault, Harvey, and many others have pointed out, if we don't have time in our day or are so numb to our daily condition that there is no opportunity of thinking "the possible," we are lost. "Good work" is both a model for and an incubator of utopian thinking.

In David Hesmondhalgh and Sarah Baker's *Creative Labour, Media Work in Three Culture Industries*[11], they, having examined all Marxist and post-structuralist analyses of ideal work, made a list of the characteristics of "good" and "bad" (as distinct from un-alienated and alienated) work. The characteristics of "good work" are: good wages, work hours, and levels of safety; autonomy; interest; sociality; self-esteem; self-realization; work-life balance; security; and making meaningful, good products. "Bad" work is the opposite of these. The possibility of such "good work" existing in the context of capitalism is exemplified by the work of Peter Drucker, "the man who invented corporate society," who was the guru of corporate management from the 50's through to the 80's, and was one of the first to identify "the knowledge industry" and its unique implications. In this "post-capitalist society", "knowledge workers" *own* the means of production; corporations are no longer "too thing focused," managers prepare for "planned abandonment," and the organization doesn't rest on yesterday's successes, and embraces destabilization. The goal of organizational management, Drucker stated, is to recognize that the most valuable resource is the worker (the most flexible and intelligent component of the system) and to acknowledge that the real business of business is "not how to do things right but how to find the right thing to do."

Erik Olin Wright, again, in his *Classes*, says it becomes

necessary to think through what it means to struggle positively for socialism rather than simply against capitalism." He uses the term "radical democratization" to describe a redistribution of organization assets through democratization of the process of control and co-operation of production. He also makes the basis for his approach to class identification and social change. As he puts it, organization-assets exploitation would continue and upon that exploitation a new structure of class relations would be built. Socialism, he points out, has to be appealing and emphasize a range of interests other than individual consumption to take over; it has to push quality of life, expansion of real freedoms, reduction of violence—in other words, provide a basis for building class coalitions for socialist objectives.[12]

Harvey describes the confluence of capitalism and emancipatory agendas in his observation that capitalism is good at constructing the institutions that mediate, necessarily, between particulars (individual aspirations) and universals (agreed upon rights) and that any radical politics needs to follow this example.[13] The value that he puts on institutions lies not only in their ability to make the particular universal but the fact that utopianism is a central part to the success of dominant social models: a "violent utopianism" helps the successful institution be both secure and open to change, as both Jefferson and Mao recognized.

It is hard to believe that any of the institutions that are meant to support architecture in the United States—the AIA, NAAB, NCARB—offer either security or utopian-motivated changability; nor have they ability to redirect legal or governmental institutions in a manner supportive to our utopian potential. The Justice Department's threat of suing the AIA under the Sherman Anti-Trust act cripples the AIA from any discussion of altering architectural fees or advocating against professional precarity;[14] the AIA shapes the contracts between architects and owners in order to avoid any risk, dutifully feeding the legal profession as it emasculates our potential relevance; the AIA sets the requirements that ensure that NAAB measures not social relevance or innovative collaborative work methods, but the prosaic criteria of structural competency and professional etiquette. These institutions need to be discarded and we need to start over. Replace the AIA with a union; de-professionalize architecture, doing away with NCARB and NAAB; get rid of contracts that pit constructors against architects and replace them with trust agreements that allow both to share risks and rewards with the owner.

D. Who is in control of the architectural agenda?

So who controls the architectural agenda? The answer is complex. From outside the discipline, developers doing capitalism's work; the public that waivers between its obsession with starchitects and its distain for the expense we add to the building process; the media that paints a picture of a profession that feeds both developer logic and public ignorance. From inside the profession, those above named institutions that ensure we are precarious, impotent, underpaid, and disrespected except in the form of fame; offices still adhering to authoritarian structures that deny the creative potential of their staff to emerge and remain pleased to have any work. As Olin Erik Wright has pointed out in his *Classes*, authorities like architects are compromised because they have ambiguous "class" allegiances; being oppressed from above by their clients they still identify with them more than their staff, making them resistant to change from below.[15]

From academia, there is a better outlook. More and more, even if the profession doesn't pay attention anymore, the students are alert to those studios that teach unconventional design methods with more collaborative, socially-motivated, or industry-connected outcomes. "Research" studio/labs might have become a cliché, but they nevertheless point to a model of design and practice that is knowledge, not form based, and include the social viability of the program as one of its parameters.[16]They are drawn to seminars that provide alternative modes of defining the discipline.[17] The students who are coming into our architecture schools and the profession are agitating. They have drunk the cool-aid of the reach of social media, the possibility of the autonomy that comes with technical virtuosity, the money that venture capitalists feed IT start-ups. They think this is cool. We can be cynical about this but it creates an expectation of a new "possible".[18] They want to sit at the table of power; they are impatient for impact. They might be awed by the forms that Zaha Hadid spreads across the globe, but they are smart enough to see that the instant cities being built in the emirates are neither urban nor public. The current situation of "produsage" creates, dialectically, the conditions that will instigate its own transformation from serving capitalism to serving social good.

So I place my bet for the future on the students. We theorists and academics must do our utmost to direct them in the right socially-motivated emancipatory direction. We need to arm them with the aggression to demand that both the nature and the product of architectural work should change. We need with every course, every publication, with every lecture, with all of our work, to persuade.[19]

Conclusion

As outlined above the hope for an emancipatory architecture rests on transforming our approach to class, technology, institutions, and students. This is a wide set of operatives. But looking at these in the context of architectural work makes that manageable. Indeed, the sorry nature of our discipline in all these regards has its benefits. Where other professions have long ago figured out there work-fee-management position in capitalism—doctors and lawyers have no fear in adopting a service model of work, managing and charging accordingly—architecture's work-aphasia is to our benefit. We have no intact model to undo; we can start ideally, getting it right the first time, now.

Yale University, where I teach, conducted a multi-year, multi-project research project into persuasive communication showing, amongst other things, that the messages should not appear to be designed to persuade; that the audience should be the in the 18-25 age range; that the speaker should be credible and attractive to the audience, should present two-sided arguments, (refuting the 'wrong' argument, of course), and distract the audience during the persuasion.[20] Perfect. We can do this. Let's go for it.

4

On The Impossibility of an Emancipatory Architecture: The Deadlock of Critical Theory, Insurgent Architects, and the Beginning of Politics

Erik Swyngedouw

... the impressive design of contemporary architecture acts as the aesthetic replacement of a lost collective myth, an attempt to infuse thaumaturgy in an era that even artists have forgotten how to dream about alternatives.[1]
—Maria Kaika

There is a shift from the model of the *polis* founded on a centre, that is, a public centre, or *agora*, to a new metropolitan spatialisation that is certainly invested in a process of *de-politicisation*.[2]
—Giorgo Agamben

The thesis of this essay is rather straightforward. Architecture cannot be an emancipatory project; it never was and never will be. Of course, such entrée seems to merely replicate Manfredo Tafuri's now already 45 year-old claim of architecture's emancipatory impossibility. However, his analysis focused on a particular theorization of architecture's ideological functioning within the reproduction of capitalism, one that considered ideology as a mystifying veil draped over the realities of capitalist life, and largely ignored the incoherence, tensions, political possibilities, frictions, and heterogeneities that cut through the forces animating the self-expansion of capital. In particular, his thesis disavowed the possibility of political events and processes of emancipatory political subjectivation—and their architectonic performativity—that occasionally traverse the fantasy of capital's impossible transgression and point towards a horizon beyond the existent. What is required today is a re-articulation of the performativity of ideology, to foreground the place of 'the political' in emancipatory politics and the process of becoming a political subject. While architecture cannot be an emancipatory project, architects, just like any other space-altering and space-forming practitioners, can and do co-animate political events and inscribe themselves in emancipatory political sequences.

As we shall argue below, over the past few years or so, insurgent architects have signaled how the political might re-emerge as an immanent practice within the production of urban space. They became political subjects in particular historical-geographical conjunctures, and through their fidelity to an emancipatory political sequence, militant activists in the unfolding of a universalizing procedure of emancipatory change. In the process, they reconsider and re-articulate their allocated function and location within the partition of the sensible and the social and technical divisions of labor. The process of becoming an insurgent architect cannot be theorized substantively—it is a process that ultimately resides in shedding the straight-jacket of the place one occupies within the social edifice by making a wager on the truth of the emancipatory process, enrolling the will to its spatialization, and mobilizing the courage of choosing sides in agonistic political encounters. Ultimately, emancipatory politics is fundamentally about transgressing the ideological fantasy that structures the reality of late-capitalist life.

We do not conceive here of ideology as some sort of illusion covering a hidden truth, waiting to be unmasked by the master truth-producers of critical theory. This was ultimately Tafuri's position. I would argue that ideology today—as Slavoj Žižek keeps reminding us—is precisely what structures reality. Žižek summarizes this most eloquently in the statement: 'despite the fact we know very well the condition we are in, still, we act as if we do not know'. Ideology is not an illusionary veil; on the contrary, it is the actual support of the real of life. We do know that capitalism is hegemonic and unequal, that architects dwell in the deadlock between artistic independence and acting as lackeys of the king, that capitalist urbanity is unsustainable, that money rules the production of space, etc... All this is well known, clear for all to see, the openly declared truth of the situation, one well rehearsed by our critical theories. We know that relations of domination and exclusion along class, gender, ethnic and a range of other power axes suture capitalist architecture and urbanity. We do know, even before Tafuri systematized this, that architecture, of necessity, provides a fantasmic support for the status quo to make sure that nothing really changes despite recurrent appeals to the 'shock of the new'. This is the Real ideological deadlock today. Cynicism today, therefore, does not reside in the dominant architectural practice of cosmopolitan elite starchitecture—their key protagonists and theoretical articulators fully endorse the position they are in; the real cynicism today resides in much of critical theory itself, utterly reveling in the negative dialectic of critique, largely without articulation of the vibrant insurgent architectural practices visible and lived in the interstitial spaces of imperial and cosmopolitan global urbanization or in the radical ega-libertarian political experimentations already present in both theory and practice. The ultimate aim of politics is intervention, to change the given socio-environmental ordering in a certain manner; it is the architectural practice *par excellence*. Like any intervention, this is a violent act, erases at least partly what is there in order to erect something new and different.

Emancipatory politics cannot be other than a practice, a set of affective and sequential acts that require painstaking organization, careful thought, radical imagination, and—above all—the intellectual and political will to inaugurate an equal, solidarity-based and free socio-spatial order that abolishes what exists and produces the new within the interstices of the old. This is actually the definition of communism that Marx and Engels already provided in *The German Ideology*: "Communism is for us not a state of affairs which is to be established, an ideal to which reality will have to adjust itself. We call communism the real movement which abolishes the present state of things."[3] The historically enduring, but presently utterly disavowed, markers of such emancipatory political sequence revolve around the notions of equality, freedom, solidarity, and the ega-libertarian management of the socio-ecological commons of life. This has become particularly acute as present-day financialized capitalist dynamics revolve precisely around the private appropriation of collective and common intellectual, affective, and cognitive powers as well as of nature's wealth and other commons of life (of which urban space is the greatest *oeuvre*), in search of rent and accumulation by dispossession.

An emancipatory alternative, in contrast, must be infinitely inclusive in its political egalitarianism and, therefore, violently exclusive to those who embrace identitarian, privatized, or other forms of historical and geographical closure of the commons, both affective and material. The political signifier that histori-cally stood for this desire, is communism. Equality, solidarity, freedom and collective mobilization of the commons by all and for all, the metonymic enchainment that quilts some meaning for communism, are today the disavowed metaphors that nonetheless still stand as foundational gestures for an emanci-patory sequence. Yet, they have been largely scripted out of the sophisticated treatises of critical thought, particularly as the collapse of existing socialism, the triumph of market capitalism, and the rise of identity politics colluded to render the very idea of communism taboo, despite its enduring subversive appeal. They have been banned by de-politicized governance arrange-ments that organize the post-political management of the givens of the situation. In an age in which presumably everything can be discussed, dissected, and represented, the common, egalitarian, and democratic making of our life world, the very foundation of architecture, has been censored, relegated to the dustbin of history. It is precisely within this situation that an intellectual and practical project of and for re-founding an emancipatory political sequence needs to be situated.

In this essay, we shall consider first the deadlock of critical urban-architectural thought today. Second, we shall argue that much of contemporary critical architectural and urban theorization is an integral part of this deadlock as critical theory has systematically disavowed thinking the political and drawing the consequences from such thought. Critical urban and architectural theory and its cynical disavowal of 'the political' over the past few decades is part and parcel of the particular process of de-politicization that has been defined and conceptualized as post-politicization.[4] Finally, we shall argue that the incipient return of insurgent urban architects as manifested in recent urban politicizing uprisings may tentatively open a space for thinking through and acting on the necessity for a new socio-spatial order articulated around the disavowed signifiers of equality, freedom, solidarity and common management of the commons.

The In-between Spaces of Hope

In his most accomplished manifesto for a radical politics of and for the city, *Spaces of Hope*, the pre-eminent theorist of capitalist urbanity, David Harvey interrogates the thorny relationship between utopias and emancipatory urban political projects.[5] He distinguishes between two dominant modes of utopian thinking and practice: utopias of spatial form and utopias of time. The former have traditionally been the staple of modernist architectural thought and practice. Consider, for example, the long lineage from Fourrier and Owen, to Le Corbusier, the Situationists, or Archigram. In the political domain, the stale utopias of spatial form associated with once existing state socialism in Eastern Europe or, for that matter, the bio-regionalist and localist dreams of various exclusive identitarian utopias, both of a leftist and rightist bend, are today invariably and correctly critiqued for their homogenising and totalising closure. In such de-politicized utopias of spatial form, difference, heterogeneity, agonistic encounter, and contestability are customarily foreclosed, ultimately leading to a presumably consensual but illusionary inclusion of all in liberal participatory governance of the givens or to an ultra-political position of radical antagonism between insider and outsiders, between friends and enemies. In the absence of recognition of the antagonisms that cut through the social, violence is, of necessity, structurally inscribed in such utopias.

Equally disturbing, if possibly even more perverse, are the utopias of time. They unfold through the promise of a fully inclusive future, which will never arrive as the in-egalitarian Real of the actually existing world invariably exceeds the fantasies of the idealised process imagined by the master-dreamers of such utopias-to-come. Cosmopolitan neo-liberalism is precisely such a utopia of process whereby the promises of the elites ('hang in there while following our guiding fantasies, we are your desire; the future will be a free, egalitarian and inclusive pluralist world of happy and equitable commodity exchange) foreshadow a rose-spectacled future that is nonetheless radically perverted in its actually existing spatialization and associated geographies of combined and uneven inclusion and exclusion. Such utopias keep things discursively radically open and the promise alive, articulated around the drive of tomorrow's ultimate realization of today's unfulfilled dreams, whereby the promise of eventual *jouissance* is postponed forever. Nonetheless, hope for the disenfranchised is desperately kept alive by the master-weavers of the utopia of time to avoid anger, despair, and rancour to boil over in abyssal violence. As such, utopias of time produce a schizophrenic subject, haunted by desires sustained by a continuous patching up of the gap between discourse and reality, ultimately nurturing a politics that perpetuates frustration while at the same time disavowing the perversities of the actually existing present.

In stark contrast to the deadlock of utopias of spatial form and of time, for Harvey, a radical emancipatory utopianism has to be a dialectical one that considers the grounding of social process in spatial form. Such spatio-temporal utopias maintain the dialectic between process and thing, between nurturing radical openness while recognizing the inevitability of temporary spatial closure. This is a process that negotiates carefully the cliff between the desire for infinite egalitarian inclusiveness and formless openness, while staring in the face, fully endorsing, the inevitable violence inscribed in temporary closure. Fully avowing this tension is precisely the terrain on which a radical emancipatory architecture is situated, the terrain where insurgent architects meet in rebel cities to carve out, experiment with, and tentatively explore the spatialized contours of more egalitarian forms of urban life.[6] This decidedly politicizing perspective cuts through the deadlock (or crisis) in which contemporary architecture and other organized space-forming activities and disciplines (like design, planning, urban management) dwell, and that has been repeated ad nauseam ever since Manfredo Tafuri's incisive—but politically impotent—insight that architecture unfolds in the impossible space of insisting on its autonomous (if not Autistic to use Maria Kaika's perceptive indictment[7]) artistic character on the one hand and its obligation to produce technically sound and socially functional environments on the other.

The deadlock of emancipatory architecture today resides not only in the recognition of, but also in perversely relishing, the iron cage of this condition. It is precisely the repetition of the mantra of its schizophrenic but apparently inescapable location that renders architecture's narrative particularly effective in supporting the ideological fantasy upon which neo-liberal cosmopolitan capitalism thrives, while disavowing at the same time not only the Real of Capital as an inherently contradictory and crisis-ridden, conflicting and contested 'thing', but—more problematically—also the immanent possibilities of emancipatory re-politicization. The repetition of the deadlock demonstrates critical architecture's failure to transgress the fantasy and seek the openings that point to a horizon beyond the actual by continuing to lament the present. Transgressing the ideological fantasy that permits architecture to cover up the negative emptiness of its own foundational core does require emancipatory architects to re-engage with the political moments that already brew in the interstices of actually existing urban practices; places where a large number of insurgent architects are already prefiguring new forms and modes of living in common that point towards an embryonic re-politicization.

The Deadlock of Left Urban Critique: Lessons from Insurgent Architects

Alain Badiou has argued recently that we are living in "a time of riots".[8] Since the magical year 2011, a seemingly never-ending proliferation of urban rebellions, sparked off by a variety of conditions, and unfolding against the backdrop of very different historical and geographical contexts, profoundly disturbed the apparently cozy neo-liberal status quo and disquieted cultural, economic and political elites. There is an uncanny choreographic affinity between the eruptions of discontent in cities as diverse as Istanbul, Cairo, Tunis, Athens, Madrid, Lyon, Lisbon, Rome, New York, Tel Aviv, Chicago, London, Berlin, Thessaloniki, Santiago, Rio de Janeiro, Stockholm, Barcelona, Montreal, Oakland, Sao Paulo, and Bucharest, metonymically enchained through distinct urban signifiers like Ghezi Park, Paternoster Square, Plaza del Sol, Tahrir Square, Plaza de la Catalunya, Syntagma Square, Green Square, Zucotti Park. These incipient

political movements staged—albeit in often inchoate, contradictory, unarticulated, and by no-means universally emancipatory manners—a profound discontent with the present state of
affairs and choreographed tentatively modes of urban being-in-
common through prolonged moments of actively constructing
new spatialities of encounter and engagement. The heterogeneous gatherers were outraged by and expose the variegated
'wrongs' and spiraling inequalities of autocratic neo-liberalization and instituted post-democratic governance. Nonetheless,
in absence of a progressive project, it is those who pursue a
political image articulated around exclusive national or ethnic
identitarian fantasies, often combined with decidedly in-egalitarian and undemocratic political visions, that generally have
most successfully capitalized politically on such outbursts of
anti-elite mass sentiment. A politics articulated around a
localized *ethnos* rather than an infinitely inclusive *demos* seems to
offer today the most performative and mobilizing conduit for
articulating a political alternative.[9]

These spectacular, decidedly urban—albeit ephemeral—
outbursts of political desires exploded alongside the proliferation
of more enduring, slow, often less visible and certainly marginalized, socio-spatial and socio-ecological experimentations with
new forms of living together. These creative forms of producing
urbanity are also visible in the insurgent practices of renewed
citizenship and innovative architectural practices for
constructing life in common beyond bare life by the majority of
the world's 'slum dwellers' and others whose 'precarious'
existence is as much part of the present urban conditions as the
cathedrals of a new architectural sublime. Do these practices and
experiments not call for an urgent reconsideration of both urban
theory and architectural praxis? Does their acting not signal a
clarion call to return the architectural intellectual gaze to
consider again what the polis has always been, namely the site
for political encounter and place for enacting the new, the

improbable, things often considered impossible by those who do not wish to see any change, the site for experimentation with, the staging and production of new radical imaginaries for what urban democratic being-in-common might be all about and what forms it might take?

Much of today's 'Critical' theory has become an integral and necessary part of the phantasmagoric ideological imaginary that structures neo-liberal urban reality itself. As architectural practices function as the marker in the making of spectacular, creative, dynamic, market-driven, 'sustainable', global urbanities that serve the cosmopolitan (neo-)liberal (and not so liberal) urban elite, critical theory, while remaining fashionably 'radical' in its representational frame, has indeed found its destiny as integral part of the intellectual and cultural support structure of this neo-liberal fantasy along with its multi-cultural and multi-vocal inclusivity.

Much of the recent history of critical urban and architectural theory has been marked by a commitment to a politics of emancipatory transformation and to the creation of socially just urban geographies. Emblematically initiated by the seminal Marxist contributions of, among many others, David Harvey, Henri Lefebvre, and Manual Castells, and architecturally inflected by Manfredo Tafuri, these perspectives reframed and transgressed how 'emancipatory' urban theory ought to be done, and what kind of urbanism and architecture can and ought to be practiced. Implicit and occasionally explicit references to normative notions of equality, justice, and freedom motivated the impulse to further the formation of a genuinely humanising urbanity and architecture. Of course, during the 1960s and 1970s, these theoretical expeditions articulated with strong and often well-organized and politically performative left organizations, many of which have today either disappeared (at least in the Global North) or surrendered to the presumably inevitable task of post-politicizing management of the neo-liberal status quo.

The epistemological and ontological parameters of what constitutes 'properly' critical emancipatory enquiry and politics have changed, as have the contours and dynamics of capitalist urbanization itself. Many of the theoretical and philosophical foundations of critical thought have been re-examined, re-formulated and often radically changed as an early emphasis on class and the political-economy of capitalist class-based urbanization has been gradually extended to include (or be replaced by) a wider range of other, often competing, theoretical accounts and political claims, most notably around identitarian inscriptions like race, ethnicity, age, sexual preference, ability, sub-alterity and gender. Surprisingly, however, relatively little critical reflection has been devoted to what constitutes the urban political domain, to what 'the political' is or where it might be located, or how to think an emancipatory political sequence after the disintegration of really existing socialism.[10]

In most of critical urban theoretical apparatuses, the political is usually assumed to emerge from what I would call a broadly 'socio-spatial' analysis. Put simply, a critical theory of the 'social' is considered to be the foundational basis from which an emancipatory urban politics can (or will) emerge, both theoretically and practically. It is the socio-spatial condition and the excavation of the procedures of its production that opens up and charts the terrain of political intervention and animates the politicizing subject. Substantive critical social theory, whether Marxist or post-Marxist, structural or post-structural, essentialist or non-essentialist, centred or decentred, presumably opens the terrain for proper political intervention and action. And every twist and turn in the meanderings of critical theory over the last few decades prefigured its own privileged transformative political subject with its socio-spatially constituted tactics: the proletarian for Marxists, woman for feminists, the creative class/cosmopolitan multitude for (neo-)liberals, the subaltern for post-colonial theorists, heterogeneously assembled human/post-human *actants* for Latourians, rhizomatic nomadic networks for Deleuzians, the symbolically inscribed body of the barred subject for Lacanians. From these, presumably 'left', perspectives, the political is seen as an emergent field that derives from substantive analysis and actually existing inscriptions: politically correct tactics flow from theoretically correct analysis that exposes the in-egalitarian dynamics of the urban condition. Such analysis continues to situate the intellectual, Plato's philosopher-king, in the driver's seat of radical urban politics.

But while critical urban thought proliferated, the neo-liberal onslaught not only radically transformed the practices and processes that shaped the urban process but also extended and intensified already deeply seated inequalities. Andy Merrifield argues that this globalization of urbanization (what Lefebvre termed *planetary urbanization*) calls for an urgent re-appraisal of urban theory and a re-visiting of the socio-spatial practices that choreograph urban inequalities as a necessary foundation for imagining new progressive politics.[11] Neil Brenner too has recently made an impassionate and urgent plea to re-visit urban theory in light of the twenty first century urbanization processes. He insists that the formulation of an emancipatory urban politics today requires a revised theorization that is adequate to the contemporary urban condition and urges us to re-think its contours as planetary urbanization has supplanted older forms of the urban and requires updated critical engagements:

[t]he nature of the structural constraints on emancipatory forms of social change, and the associated imagination of alternatives to capitalism have been qualitatively transformed through the acceleration of geo-economic integration, the intensified financialization of capital, the crisis of the post-war model of welfare state intervention, the still ongoing neo-liberalization of state forms and the deepening of planetary ecological crises.[12]

He concludes that "the challenge for those committed to the project of critical theory is to do so in a manner that is adequate to the continued forward-motion of capital, its associated crisis-tendencies and contradictions, and the struggles and oppositional impulses it is generating across the variegated landscapes of the world economy."[13] While I am broadly in agreement with this call for a transformed critical urban theory, I maintain that a program that insists on furthering substantive theory as a prerequisite for emancipatory urban transformation functions today as an integral part of the process of post-politicization. Such effort constitutes, after the collapse of Master narratives, nothing less than a response to the University's injunction to be critical and liberally progressive. I concur here with Žižek that theoretical critique is not only fully accounted for, it is actually positively invited and has become one of the decisive legitimizing *dispositifs* of the current phase of neo-liberalization.

In contrast to this, I contend that there is nothing that can any longer be done with critical urban or architectural theory as a basis for re-centring the emancipatory political. The various insurgent urban politicizing movements that dot the landscape of planetary urbanism testify precisely to the bankruptcy of critical urban thought and urge us to think 'the political' again as an immanent field of action. Indeed, for Alain Badiou, socio-economic "analysis and politics are absolutely disconnected": the former is a matter for expertise and implies hierarchy; the latter is not. An absolute separation has to be maintained, he argues, between "science and politics, of analytic description and political prescription."[14] Much of critical theory can at best be oppositional, operate within the standard contestation of 'democratic' rule, but cannot think political transformation.[15]

For Badiou (as well as Jacques Rancière), the democratic political is not a reflection of something else, like the cultural, the social, or the economic. Instead, it is the axiomatic affirmation of the egalitarian capacity of each and all to act politically. It is a site open for occupation by those who call it into being, claim its occupation and stage 'equality' in the face of the actually existing inequalities that mark the state of the situation, irrespective of the 'place' they occupy within the social edifice. It is manifested in the process of subjectivation, in the 'passage to the act' by militants in a militant organization, operating at a distance of the state, and by their fidelity to a communist horizon.

Post-politicization and the incipient return of the political

The people are those who, refusing to be the population, disrupt the system.[16]

—Michel Foucault

Re-thinking the political is vital, I maintain, for an emancipatory architectural project in a contemporary urban condition that is characterized by a post-politicizing police order that manages the spatial allocation, distribution and circulation of things and people through a consensually agreed and naturalized neo-liberal arrangement The political as a space for nurturing (political) dissensus is thereby foreclosed.[17] These techno-managerial practices and procedures colonize and evacuate the political from everyday space.[18] Spatialized policies (planning, architecture, urban policies, etc.) are among the core *dispositifs* of such post-politicizing governing. Post-politicization is a process by which a consensus has been built around the inevitability of state-backed capitalism as an economic system, parliamentary democracy as the political ideal, humanitarianism and inclusive cosmopolitanism as its moral foundation. Such consensual bio-political governmentality either disavows fundamental conflict or elevates it to the violence of antithetical ultra-politics.

The post-political consensus is therefore one that is radically reactionary, one that forestalls the articulation of divergent, conflicting and alternative trajectories of future urban possibilities and assemblages. Consensus does not equal peace or absence of fundamental conflict,[19] but disavows, if not forecloses, the inherent antagonisms inscribed in the self-expansion of value in capitalist circuits of production and exchange. This retreat of the political into the cocoon of consensual policy-making within a singular distribution of the givens of the situation constitutes the zero ground of politics. Something similar is, of course, at work in the micro-politics of local urban struggles, dispersed resistances and alternative practices that suture much of the field of 'traditional' urban social movements today. These are the spheres where an urban activism dwells as some form for 'placebo'-politicalness.[20] This anti-political impulse works through colonization of the political by the social through sublimation. It elevates disagreements, contestations and fractures that inevitably erupt out of the incomplete saturation of the social world by the police order to the dignity of political interruption. For example, the variegated, dispersed and often highly effective (on their own terms) forms of urban activism and movements that emerge within concrete localized socio-spatial interventions, such as, among others, around land-use, local pollution problems, road proposals and transport issues, urban development schemes, architectural projects, airport noise or expansions, the felling of trees, the construction of incinerators, industrial works, the dispossession of the commons of land, air, or water, etc... elevate localized particular groups and/or organizations to the level of the political, but without universalizing aspirations. These particular forms of hysterical acting-out become imbued with political significance. The space of the political is thereby "reduced to the seeming politicization of these groups... Here the political is not truly political because of the restricted nature of the constituency."[21] Rather than politicizing, such social colonization of the political in fact erodes and outflanks the political dimension of ega-libertarian universalization. The latter cannot be substituted by a proliferation of identitarian, multiple, and ultimately fragmented communities. Moreover, such expressions of protest, which are framed fully within the existing practices and police order are, in the current post-political arrangement, already fully acknowledged—if not actively invited—and accounted for.

Emancipatory politicization, in contrast, re-frames what is regarded as political. It inaugurates the re-partitioning of the logic of the police, the re-ordering of what is visible and audible, and registers as voice what was only registered as noise. It occurs in places not allocated to the exercise of power or the instituted negotiation of recognized differences and interests. As Badiou insists, politics emerges as an event in the singular act of choreographing egalitarian appearance of being-in-common that unfolds at a distance from the State. The political is, therefore, about enunciating dissent and rupture. It is literally about voicing speech that claims a place in the order of things, demanding "the part for those who have no-part."[22] It is the arena in which the anarchic noise of the rabble (the part of no-part)—the excluded, disenfranchised, precarious, undocumented, marginalized—is turned into the recognized voice of the People. The political is, therefore, always disruptive. It emerges with the "refusal to observe the 'place' allocated to people and things."[23] It is the terrain where the axiomatic democratic principle of equality is tested in the face of a wrong experienced by "those who have no part." Politically, "[e]quality is not something to be researched or verified by critical or other social theory or philosophy but a principle to be upheld."[i4] Equality is neither some sort of utopian longing (as is implicit in much of critical urban and architectural theory) nor a sociological concept that can be verified and tested ex-post. It is, in contrast, the very condition upon which the democratic political is contingently and axiomatically founded. The political becomes, for Žižek and Rancière, the space of litigation,[25] the space of those who are not-All, who are uncounted and unnamed, but in their acting stage and demonstrate equality.

Designing dissensus

Localised resistance as the ultimate horizon of urban movements is nothing but a hysterical acting out; a subterfuge that masks what is truly at stake—making sure that nothing really changes. In contrast, the insurgent architects I mentioned above point to a horizon, a possibility, beyond resistance. While staging equality in public squares is a vital moment, the process of transformation requires the slow but unstoppable production of new forms of spatialization quilted around materializing the claims of equality, freedom and solidarity. In other words, what is required now and what needs to be thought through is if and how these proto-political insurgent events can turn into a spatialized political 'truth' procedure. This raises the question of political subjectivation and organizational configurations, and requires perhaps forging a new political Name that captures the imaginary of and desire for an ega-libertarian commons appropriate for the twenty first century's planetary urbanization.

During the nineteenth and twentieth centuries, these names were closely associated with 'communism' or 'socialism', and centered on the key tropes of the party as adequate organizational form, the proletarian as privileged political subject, the state as the arena of struggle and site to occupy, and the inscription of a wide range of social and professional activities, including architecture, design, and planning, within its organizational and performative orbit. It dwelt in the impossible space of distance from the state while adhering to a state-centered project. However, state, party, and proletarian may no longer be the key axes around which an emancipatory sequence might become performative. Considerable intellectual work needs to be done and all manner of experimentation is required in terms of thinking through and pre-figuring what organizational forms are appropriate and adequate to this task, what constitutes the terrain of struggle, and what or who are the agents of its enactment?

The urgent tasks now to undertake for those who maintain fidelity to the political events choreographed in the new insurrectional spaces revolve centrally around inventing new modes and practices of collective and sustained political mobilization, organizing the concrete modalities of spatializing and universalizing the Idea provisionally materialized in these intense and contracted localized insurrectional events and the assembling of a wide range of new political subjects (irrespective of their location within the social edifice) who are not afraid to stage an egalitarian being-in-common, imagine a different commons, demand the impossible, perform the new and confront the violence that will inevitably intensify as those who insist on maintaining the present order realize that their days might be numbered. Such post-capitalist politics is not and cannot be based solely on class positions. As Marx asserted, class is a bourgeois concept and practice. The insurgencies are not waged by a class, but by the masses as an assemblage of heterogeneous political subjects. It is when the masses as a political category stage their presence that the elites recoil in horror.

For Alain Badiou, "a change of world is real when an inexistent of the world starts to exist in the same world with maximum intensity."[26] The order of the sensible is shaken, and the kernel for a new common sense, a new mode of being in common becomes present in the world and makes its presence common-sens(e)ible. It is the appearance of another world in the world. This is precisely what the sprawling urban insurgents and rebellions have achieved, by igniting a new sensibility about the polis as a democratic and potentially democratizing space. The tidal wave of urban protests shattered the post-political idyll of an unfractured society that recognizes the identitarian claims and demands of its members and organizes a consensually negotiated democratic compromise without any remainders. These protests stand for the dictatorship of the democratic—direct and egalitarian—against the despotism of the 'democracy' of the elites—representative and inegalitarian.[27]

The urban insurgents turned the particular grievances that ignited the events into a wholesale attack on the instituted order, on the unbridled commodification of urban life in the interests of the few, on the unequal choreographies of actually existing representational democracy. The particular demands transformed seamlessly into a universalizing staging for something different, however diffuse, inchoate and unarticulated this may presently be. The assembled groups ended up without particular demands and thereby demanded everything, nothing less then the transformation of the instituted order. They staged new ways of practicing equality and democracy, experimented with innovative and creative ways of being together in the city, and prefigured, both in practice and in theory, new ways of distributing goods, accessing services, producing healthy environments, managing space, constructing artifacts, organizing debate, managing conflict, being-in-common, practicing ecologically saner life-styles, and negotiating urban space in an emancipatory manner.

In the aftermath of these insurgencies, a range of new sociospatial practices are experimented with, from housing occupations and movements against dispossession in Spain to experimenting with new ega-libertarian life-styles and forms of social and ecological organization in Greece and many other places, alongside more traditional forms of political organizing. An extraordinary experimentation with dispossessing the dispossessor, with reclaiming the commons and organizing access, transformation and distribution in more ega-libertarian ways marks the return to 'ordinary' life in the aftermath of the insurgencies. These incipient ideas materialize in a variety of places and practices, in the midst of painstaking efforts to build alliances, bridge sites, repeat the insurgencies, establish connectivities and, in the process, produce organization and generalize desire. Such procedures demand painstaking organization, sustained political action, militant organization, imaginative urban designs, and a committed fidelity to universalizing the egalitarian trajectory for the management of the commons.

The recognition that political acts are singular interventions that produce particular socio-ecological arrangements and in doing so foreclose the possibility of others to emerge, is of central importance. Any intervention enables the formation of certain assemblages and closes down others. The 'violence' inscribed in such choice has to be fully endorsed. For example, one cannot have simultaneously a truly carbon-free city and permit unlimited car-based mobility. They are mutually exclusive. Even less can an egalitarian, democratic, solidarity-based and ecologically sensible urban future be produced without marginalizing or excluding those who insist on a private appropriation of the commons of the earth, the uneven distribution of rents through financialized circuits of capital, and the mobilization of the commons for accumulation and personal enrichment.

Such violent encounters always constitute a political act, one that can be legitimised only in political terms, and not—as is customarily done—through an externalised legitimation that resides in a fantasy of a cohesive city, an 'emancipatory' architecture, or 'sustainable' urban design practice. Any political or architectural act is one that re-orders socio-ecological co-ordinates and patterns, reconfigures uneven socio-ecological relations, often with unforeseen or unforeseeable, consequences. It expresses a choice, takes sides, invariably signals a totalitarian moment and the temporary suspension of the democratic understood as the agonistic encounter of heterogeneous views under the aegis of an axiomatically presumed equality of all. The gap between the democratic moment, predicated upon the presumption of the equality and the autocratic moment as the (temporary suspension of the democratic) needs to be radically endorsed. Avowing this might cut through the deadlock of architecture today. While the democratic political, founded on a presumption of equality, insists on difference, disagreement, radical openness, and exploring multiple possible futures, concrete spatial-ecological intervention is necessarily about relative closure (for some), definitive choice, singular intervention and, thus, certain exclusion and occasionally even outright silencing.

While the negative dialectic mobilized by critical thought over the past two decades usurped the will for radical change, the return of the emancipatory hypothesis contained in the Idea of Communism (or shall we call it Commonism?) requires a new courage of the architectural intellect to break down barriers and taboos, to dare to think universalizing emancipatory politics again, to trust the demands formulated by those that have no voice and no part, to trust the will for change and to embrace the task of testing radically the truth of the communist hypothesis; a truth that can only be established through a new emancipatory political sequence. The communist hypothesis forces itself onto the terrain of the political through the process of subjectivation, a coming into being through voluntarist actions, procedures and performances, of collective embodiments of fidelity to the presumption of equality and freedom. It is a fidelity to the practical possibility of communism, but without ultimate guarantee in history, geography, the party, or the state. Communism is an idea without ultimate ground, but with extraordinary emancipatory potential. The emancipatory subjects are those who assemble together, not only to demand freedom and equality but to take it, to carve out, occupy, organize—and in doing so imagine, produce, and construct—the spaces for the enactment of this politics. Emancipatory urbanity enacts and performs itself—much like the Paris communards did in 1871. It is in this way that the right to the city, to the production of this collective *ouevre*, becomes performative. Advancing this hypothesis requires serious intellectual engagement in order to tease out and tentatively symbolize what an equal, free and self-organizing urban being-in-common for the twenty first century might be all about and look like. This is a formidable task to be asked of the communist (common) architectural intellect. It will require serious theoretical reconceptualization, a restoration of trust in our theories, a courageous engagement with painful histories and geographies, and, above all, abandoning the fear of failing again. The fear of failing has become so overwhelming that fear of real change is all that is left; resistance is as far as our horizons reach—transformation, it seems, can no longer be thought, let alone practiced. As Wilson and Swyngedouw conclude their book on the political possibilities of new radical spaces:

The choice we face is a simple one. In fact, it is no choice at all. We either indulge the fantasy that what exists can be perpetuated, and seek to improve it to the best of our humanitarian abilities while lamenting theoretically its inevitable deadlock, or we begin to seriously think through the possibilities of reimagining and realizing the communist hypothesis for the twenty first century. Ironically, it is the first of these options that must be dismissed as dangerously 'utopian', in the sense that our catastrophe cannot be solved within the parameters of global capitalism. This conclusion can be posed as a question to our enemies: 'why do you keep saying there is no alternative, when there really is no alternative?[28]

Acknowledgements

I would like to thank Maria Kaika and Nadir Lahiji for their suggestions and comments on earlier drafts of the paper.

Dialogues: Round Two

5

The Misery of Theory: on Universality, Contingency, and Truth

Libero Andreotti

Theories are nothing in themselves and have only to be proven in the light of historical action
—Guy Debord

The Left, in American schools of architecture today, must be weary of what it says. While liberalism survives just enough for a semblance of open debate, anything more radical must be carefully avoided, not so much because it is unpopular or 'uncool', to borrow a term in Peggy's paper to which I will return (indeed, polls among college youth today indicate a more favorable attitude towards 'socialism' than towards 'capitalism') [1], but simply because it is well understood that such positions can be fatal to one's career. Such is the power of self-censorship to enforce what Noam Chomsky famously called "the bounds of thinkable thought". That this effort to normalize and contain dissent remains a rather precarious affair, however, is borne out by many indications, not the least of which is the sheer intensity of the propaganda needed to maintain an appearance of consensus, and by a whole new world of strange and inspiring political activism that is emerging everywhere.

I should say right away that much of what follows reflects my long absence from the States (from 1994 to 2011) and the discovery, on my return, of an academic environment completely dominated by a market fundamentalism whose well-funded reach had penetrated even into what used to be a bastion of progressive politics, architectural theory. Shifts of such magnitude, of course, are hardly confined to a single academic field, but invest many aspects of society. Several recent studies, for example, suggest a decline in empathy and social awareness among the general population, with a sharp drop among college students over the last decade (phenomena that correlate with increased isolation, TV watching and online activity, decline in reading, and economic insecurity).[2] Given this, it is interesting to consider what role, however small, theorists may have played in shaping such attitudes within architecture schools, and how they might also work to counter them.

Of the three contributions I have been asked to review— David's *Architecture, the Built and the Idea of Socialism*, Peggy's *Architects, Really*, and Erik's *On the Impossibility of Emancipatory Architecture, The deadlock of Critical Theory, Insurgent Architects, and the Beginning of Politics*—the one that addresses this wider context most directly is Erik's, and I will begin with it. Before I do, however, it is not unuseful to note how very different each essay is and how, taken together, they are characteristic of architectural theory on the Left today: no longer the tightly knit discursive enterprise it was during its heyday (say, around 1980) but a diffuse collection of viewpoints related to distinct positions like those of an activist (Erik), a philosopher (David), or an educator (Peggy). One effect of this not unwelcome diversity, however, is a pervasive uncertainty about the function, goals, and limits of theory itself. To speak of an "institutional crisis" would be to exaggerate the consistency of a field that was never all that monolithic. To speak of an "institutional crisis" would be to exaggerate the consistency of a field that was never all that monolithic. But clearly, over the last few decades, theory has been overtaken by forces that have undercut many of its assumptions and seriously challenged its status. Among them is a new wave of technology-induced neophilia that makes it very difficult to develop *any* theoretical perspective for very long—a phenomenon linked to perceptual shifts that are reconfiguring, in profound and as yet unknown ways, the human sensorium. In the face of such changes, the temptation to overdramatize is itself symptomatic, as is the talk of crisis, rupture, and epochal shifts that is the common fare of a certain type of critical discourse. Against this, it is my view that one of theory's first obligations is to set as its "absolute horizon" ethical principles as near to universal as practically possible. From this perspective, what Chomsky called the two main responsibilities of intellectuals—to understand clearly the workings of power and to imagine, and as far as possible to practice, an alternative based on a theory of human nature as best we understand it—continue to represent, in my view, as good a basis for such an effort as can be found.[3]

In what follows, aside from lending support to the many excellent points made by my colleagues, I want to focus on how each of them contributes to a re-definition of theory and of its place within the broader project of the Left. In attempting to clarify, and occasionally to question the approach of each author, I advance the view that theory is, or should be, a continuous process of rational and ethical inquiry and that its proper object should be "truth" and not persuasion. These "basic banalities" are, in a nutshell, my critical reactions to the three papers I have been asked to review.

Erik's piece, as best I can see, makes two important claims. The first is critical theory's complicity with the rise of what he negatively terms the present-day regime of 'post-politics'; the second is the need, as he puts it following Badiou and Rancière, to "remake the political an immanent practice in the production of space." This second point draws its force from the many eruptions of urban discontent that since 2011 have invested cities from Istanbul to Tel Aviv, where "insurgent architectures" are, in Erik's words, "already prefiguring new forms and modes of living in common." Erik marshals his evidence with force—so much so, in fact, that one wonders about the opening disclaimer that, in a nod to Tafuri, bluntly states: "architecture will never be and has never been a project of emancipation." Luckily, however, this turns out not to be the case and there are good reasons to believe that an "emancipatory architecture" is not only possible but real in the examples Erik brings to the table.

The greatest strength of Erik's essay, in my view, is its passionate call to action, which makes theory subservient to its practical role in the struggle. From this standpoint, which I fully endorse, theory is to be the opposite of the bland, academic theorizing that has worked for so long objectively to stifle change (in my own piece I suggested that, to some extent, Colin Rowe fits this description). Against this, Erik adopts notions from Ranciere, Žižek, and Badiou to invert many received ideas in what amounts to a counter-theoretical (or anti-theoretical) movement in which the driving force is action. While this makes for an energizing read, I find myself unsure of its theoretical foundations and unable to follow through on all of Erik's conclusions.

A central principle in Erik's essay is the idea of "the political." This follows in part from his justified critique of various forms of localized identitarian struggle in favor of what he calls a "proper political dimension of ega-libertarian universalization." The model for this idea is Rancière's notion of "emancipatory politicization", a process that "reframes" politics and inaugurates a "re-ordering" or a "redistribution" of the sensible. This is certainly an elegant way to describe the rupturing force of insurgent movements such as those Erik cites, which seem to originate outside established political institutions. However, such a formulation, in my view, is problematic in at least three ways. First, as David noted in his paper, it presents a phenomenology of the "event" that has troubling metaphysical and vitalist connotations. Secondly, it tends to dismiss existing political institutions, especially the institutions of government (according to Erik, the political is an event that, through rupture and dissent, "unfolds at a distance from the State") in a way that risks depriving "the part that has no part" of one of the few remaining instruments to resist the rule of unaccountable private power. Third, and more troubling, is Rancière's formulation of the political in terms of an abstract defence of free speech, or as he puts it, an axiomatic affirmation of "the egalitarian capacity of each and all to act" and claim a place in the political order. This strikes me as a purely formal conception that leaves out all the historically specific instances of such conflicts. How would Rancière distinguish, for example, between genuine insurgencies such as those Erik cites, and the many orchestrated rebellions, including the long list of "orange revolutions" in whose support we are constantly being enlisted? Strictly speaking, "a site open for occupation by those who call it into being", as Erik calls the political, might just as well describe the insurgent techniques of the Tea Party or of the one-time political outsiders like Newt Gingrich. As Bruno Bosteels notes, the a-historicity of Rancière's categories risks turning them into a "radicalism pivoting on its own emptiness...cut off from any inscription in a specific time and place."[4]

Aside from these questions, which might better be directed to Rancière than to Erik, I also found myself unable to agree fully with some of the essay's conclusions. For example, according to Erik, post-politics, post-criticism, and even a certain brand of disengaged ideological critique have lead to a "theoretical deadlock" today, in which architectural theory has merely become a "legitimizing *dispositif*" for neo-liberalism. While it is hard to completely disagree with this assessment, I would nevertheless still want to resist the dismissal of critical theory *tout court*, especially the tradition of "ideological critique" represented by Tafuri and others. To support his claim about the death of theory, Erik invokes Žižek's onto-Lacanian notion of ideology as a "structuring of reality", which invalidates, he maintains, the basic assumptions of ideological critique. He also cites Badiou on the inability of theory to properly "think the political" (one wonders if such a judgment would apply to Badiou). In either case, a justified desire to reject ineffectual theorizing risks, in my view, throwing out the baby with the bathwater. Would it not be better to regard ideological critique as a theoretical practice that, limited though it may be by a certain baggage of concepts, still serves an essential function in any project of the Left? Similarly, isn't it better to see Žižek's notions about ideology, including his account of how 'despite the fact that we know very well the condition we are in, we act as if we did not know', as an extended, evolving reflection on the dilemmas of political action rather than a simple replacement of the old notion of ideology as illusion?[5]

Erik's drive to overturn accepted notions on the Left can sometimes result in awkward formulations like the following about post-politics today:

[The post-political is] a process by which a consensus (is) built around the inevitability of state-backed capitalism as an economic system, on parliamentary democracy as the political ideal, and on humanitarianism and inclusive cosmopolitanism as its moral foundation.

While there is much truth in this characterization of the *pretense* of post-politics, unless the author wants to be understood as being *himself against* humanitarianism, cosmopolitanism, and parliamentary democracy, he would do best to place those terms in quotation marks. A similar problem can be found elsewhere in Erik's text, for example when he claims that "any political and architectural act ... invariably signals a *totalitarian* moment and the *temporary suspension of the democratic*" (my emphasis). Taken literally, these assertions sound like a defence of totalitarianism against humanism and democracy. The only way to avoid such absurd conclusions is to distinguish sharply between the ordinary use of common terms and the particular meaning intended by the author—who would do well, if possible, to use another term altogether. As Chomsky noted in a famous debate with Foucault, language is the field of struggle for theory and certain terms—like democracy, for example—should not be surrendered without a fight.[6]

None of my remarks are meant to question the courageous drive with which Erik denounces the involution of theory, its increasingly subservient role, its diminished ambitions, and its failure to rise up to the challenge posed, today, by the urgent need to act. Indeed, nothing, in my view, could be more important. But the misery of theory, however well deserved, cannot be allowed to turn into cynical dismissal of all forms of theorizing. What we need today is not less but *more* and *better* theory, and this is only possible through a long effort of theoretical labor, working like Hamlet's "old mole", who keeps speaking from under the stage and "goes ever on and on...until it bursts asunder the crust of earth which divided it from the sun."[7]

II

Having just taken Erik to task for discounting theory in favor of action, I shall now proceed to take on David's essay for partly the opposite reasons: for failing to consider how arguments that *in themselves* are perfectly legitimate can have very different consequences depending on the contexts in which they are deployed—in short, for neglecting tactics and timing in favor of theory. To play Erik off David in this way is perhaps unfair for a paper that is a reflexive, methodically rigorous essay by a philosopher, one of the few in the Anglo-Saxon world who are willing to engage the treacherous field of architecture, but it is just too tempting. Like Erik's, David's essay sets a high standard and I will waste no time agreeing with its well considered arguments, set out clearly according to the three sections indicated in its title, "Architecture, the Built, and the Idea of Socialism."

What I would like to draw attention to, instead, is the extremely cautious tone of his opening remarks. Their main point, it would seem, is to immunize the reader against any possibility of wishful thinking: "A critical reflection upon the 'emancipatory' potentials of architecture—David claims—depends on *"lucid and sober* accounting for 'what architects could do when certain things weren't possible and when they were'" (my emphasis). David goes on to claim that no serious consideration of the question of architecture and emancipation is possible without a prior "historical account of [architecture's] specifically modern status as an *institution*, a status which opens up an irreducible non-identity with regard to the actual material practices to which it relates, and that cannot merely be voluntaristically willed away, since it is embedded in economic, technological and legal structures that are not themselves 'architectural'."

Thus stated, the argument is unexceptionable. It follows in a long tradition of Marxist thinking centered on the dual conviction that if, on the one hand, material conditions set absolute limits to what is doable and thinkable at any one time (that 'being determines consciousness', as Marx would say) on the other, changing the world is nevertheless not only possible and necessary, but even—according to the more "scientific" strains of Marxism—inevitable and that there exists, within those material conditions, a "real movement that abolishes the present state of things."[8] For David, clearly, both are inseparable elements of a single political project. Yet it is mostly on the first set of considerations that his essay insists. Architecture's profound conditioning is evident, he says, in its problematic relation to "the built," which raises almost insurmountable theoretical difficulties in the complexity and unpredictability of even the most banal architectural tasks, as recounted by Aleandro Zaera-Polo, for example, and in the loss of effective control one sees in the recent phenomenon of authorship and 'façadism'. Even the issue of autonomy is seen by David along these lines, not according to the enlightenment ideals I argued in my paper were, and should again become, central to architectural discourse, but as an index of the inescapable realities within which architecture is condemned to operate. Tafuri and Adorno both loom large in this account, with Piranesian images of chains and iron cages recurring in both.

Stoicism, tragedy, melancholy and anguish—the recurring traits of Tafuri's writings—were all distinctive of a particular time and place, namely European Marxism of the 1970s and its stern criticism of the 60s, with their emphasis on 'juissance', 'play', and the carnivalesque. At that time, Tafuri's insistence on architecture's institutional constraints played an important role in the *defense* of Modernism against emerging right-wing critiques of social housing, form Yamasaki's Pruitt Igoe in Saint Louis (1954-76) to Rossi's Gallaratese Housing near Milan (1973). In retrospect, such a critique was especially prescient considering the fate of the latter in the US after the election of Ronald Reagan in 1980, when public housing funds began to be redirected towards an ever more massive—and profitable—prison-building program.[9]Today, however, the problem is emphatically *not* the persistence of naïve, socially progressive utopianisms, but its opposite: what Erik rightly calls a new cynicism that has abandoned all attempts to develop a socially responsible practice. In such a context, arguments about architecture's institutional constraints are more apt to be deployed to support, rather than reject, a narrowing of architecture's mission to an uncritical acceptance of the status quo—like Patrick Schumacher does, for example, when he categorically excludes questions of the political, the social and economic from the "purview" of designers, claiming that "it is not architecture's societal function to actively promote or initiate political agendas."[10] As Douglas Spencer notes, from such positions "contemporary architecture is able to release itself from any obligation to articulate an intelligible relationship to the social" and can cynically embrace any political project whatsoever, regardless of its social effects.[11]

The greatest need in architecture today, I would argue, is for ethically courageous acts that proceed from the recognition of the architect's *unavoidable* implication in social, political, and economic processes towards which one *does* have a margin of autonomy to engage and if necessary even oppose. It is in this sense that David's essential truism that "humanity makes its own history but not under conditions of its own choosing" would benefit, in my view, from another, even more basic one: the simple reminder that "designers are responsible for the predictable consequences of their actions." At a time when once-admired exponents of the avant-garde have become major actors in global financing schemes that damage the environment, violate human rights, or saddle states and communities with enormous debt, all under cover of "realistically engaging" with market forces; when architecture has become a preferred weapon in neo-liberalism's assault on cities, ecologies, and entire social systems, such a basic truism bears repeating. Besides, as Weizman notes, the time is fast approaching when architecture will be added to the list of possible crimes against humanity.[12]

This would mean, for example, adopting the equivalent of the Hippocratic oath for architects, prompting more of them to opt out of questionable commissions, giving a renewed legitimacy to the *principled refusal to cooperate* that Žižek humorously refers to as the "Bartleby strategy."[13] Such disruptive forms of abstention need not condemn one to marginality: there are many other options open to designers who refuse to engage in the business of serving unscrupulous investors. In sum, if I insist heavily on the ethical imperatives that must form the basis of any project of emancipation, it is not because David somehow forgets to consider them — indeed, the second half of this paper is unequivocal in this regard. Rather, it is because architecture's main failing today, I am convinced, comes less from an inade-quate understanding of how it is externally conditioned than from a lack of courage and moral intelligence.

III

This is exactly why Peggy's call to democratize the workplace is so timely. As economist Richard Wolff puts it, why should a society that constantly celebrates the "democratic process" in endless theatrical re-enactments make working people spend the majority of their lives in conditions—such as those governing the world of business of the modern corporation—of near complete tyranny and arbitrary authority?[14] Architectural offices, as Peggy notes, are particularly guilty of abusive, illegal, and undemocratic working practices that combine "some of the worst features of both material and immaterial labor." Hence the first obligation for any seriously emancipatory practice is to expose injustice and enact democratic reform in "our own architectural house."

The question is especially relevant since major changes in the building industry and the design professions today are introducing patterns of work that are, in many ways, even more unequal than the already lop-sided ones that used to structure architectural offices. Increasingly, as Peggy notes, graduates enter a field that offers less job security, fewer opportunities for advancement, longer hours, lower wages, and less predictable work schedules than what was available to earlier generations of designers. Despite the self-empowerment discourse of management theorists, the actual conditions of architectural labor have deteriorated to the point of being indistinguishable from those of the 'global precariat' (a term obtained by merging precarious with proletariat), or even worse, the "flexi-worker" on which the Italian autonomists have had much to say—in short, the low-paid informal work that is the permanent condition of most people on the planet today. These forms of exploitation follow directly from Reagan's and Thatcher's relentless attack on labor and trade-unions, and on the neo-liberal policies designed to cheapen the price of labor and drastically weaken its capacity for collective action. They are typical manifestations of the massive *downward shock* brought about by neo-liberalism and its subservient ideology of management, which presents insecure, unprotected employment as the solution to problems of economic growth.

It is a measure of just how far architectural theory has moved from its earlier social ideals that this very same management discourse has now penetrated deeply into the field of design education, becoming what Peggy describes as simply part of "the territory that architectural work *must* negotiate" (my emphasis). Peggy herself unfortunately exemplifies this approach by attempting to engage at least some aspects of the discourse of management around "creative labor" and the "knowledge economy". Among the latter is what she perceives as a positive thrust in the writings of Peter Drucker towards more 'open' organizational models "that shift away from object-making and standard office constructs" toward more open and democratic directions.

The appeal of this peculiar combination of traditional Left critique with management theory is not hard to explain. For one thing, as Peggy is keen to remind us, entrepreneurialism is "cool" among students and part of the task of any educator is to "construct a desire for change" by building on widely shared beliefs, no matter how repugnant they may be to the very idea of an emancipatory architecture. There is also the fact, well documented by Boltanski and Chiapello, that recent management discourse superficially incorporates much of the 1960s social critique of capitalism—including ideas like creativity, self-management, and personal freedom that are commonly invoked by various libertarian strands of free-market thinking.[15] It stands to reason that an educational effort to stimulate the student would try to build a "persuasive" case starting from these values.

The question, for me, is at what cost? No doubt many ideas

about the 'knowledge economy' are well intended, reflecting broadly progressive liberal beliefs. A recent example is Richard Florida's proselytizing about the 'creative class', with its obvious appeal to architects who are thus re-cast as the avant-garde of a more promising economic future.[16] Yet the generally progressive liberal principles that motivate this type of management literature (in Florida's case, the idea that creativity is a universally innate human trait that deserves the chance to be realized) are challenged by their unequivocal acceptance of neo-liberal capitalism and market logic as the economic context in which one is *obliged* to operate.

According to Peggy, the post-Fordist economy opens up the possibility for new and more cooperative models of work in which 'flexibility' and 'precariousness' are at least partly compensated for by a new sense of agency and empowerment. Whether these (largely imaginary?) benefits can offset the harsher realities of post-Fordist work, however, is doubtful in my view. Meanwhile, it is not irrelevant to mention Dutch art sociologist Pascal Gielen, who draws attention to how some of the new exploitative practices in the arts are turning to the architectural model of the "project"—temporary, often unpaid, intense personal investment in one-off initiatives with no guarantee of success or long-term commitment—to extract more productivity from workers.[17] Gielen writes:

The magic word these days is 'creativity.' And not just for artists: managers and policymakers alike demand creativity. Even family therapists and mediators urge us to find more creative solutions. Nowadays, creativity is all about positive morality. We expect nothing but good from it. But what remains of the meaning of the word when just about everybody is using it to death?[18]

According to Gielen, such pseudo-concepts basically serve to obscure the dominant relations of production and the conditions of exploitation that underlie the whole mythology of post-Fordist 'creative entrepreneurialism.' Their superficially progressive appeal hides a meaner ideological function which is essentially incompatible with a Left or class-based vision of radical change.

Thus, while I would certainly endorse Peggy's call for democratization of the workplace, I am less convinced about her efforts to reconcile a Left political program with the culture of business. It seems to me unlikely, for example, that the latter would ever agree to something like real collective bargaining rights for architectural workers, an idea that strikes at the heart of the Reagan assault on the working class, exposing the whole fraudulent construction on which neo-liberalism is built and which, for this reason, has little chance of being realized within the current system.

A recent example is America's long tradition of pragmatism that teaches us that it is better to focus on what contending parties have in common instead of what divides them, that compromise is necessary for persuasion, that ideas must be judged by their 'usefulness'. Perhaps it is time to question these assumptions, recognizing that the pursuit of consensus at any cost, the replacement of truth with "desirable belief" and of facts with "warranted assertions", as Alex Carey noted in his path-breaking study of corporate propaganda, is an ideological construction uniquely congenial to the public relations industry and the already inordinate power of business, with its elaborate apparatus of deceptions and illusions. As Carey notes, the "path back to truth and an honoring of the democratic rights of citizens and workers" cannot be traversed until the subject of corporate propaganda and its control on academia and in American society is faced up to squarely and historically.[19]

To return to the "basic banalities" mentioned at the start, I have tried to underline what I feel are some of the essential

challenges for theory on the Left. Among these are 1) the importance of integrating a new concepts in the tradition of ideological
critique—not only to strengthen that tradition, but also as a way
to correct a certain ahistorical tendency in the writings of Žižek,
Rancière, and Badiou; 2) the danger of ignoring the need to act in
a timely way against the ideological assaults that undermine
theory's foundations in the name of free-market realism; and 3)
the need for theorists to expose the irreducible antagonism at the
heart of any project of emancipation—a conflict that highlights
theory's unavoidably partisan nature. Together these challenges
underscore the significance, for any architecture or politics of the
left, of the *universality* of its basic principles, of the *contingency* of
its tactics, and of the *truth* of its claims—principles that are as
necessary in a practical sense as they are, however, insufficient to
guarantee the real value of *any* theory. As Guy Debord wrote:

> Theories are only made to die in the war of time. Like military
> units, they must be sent into battle at the right moment; and
> whatever their merits or insufficiencies, they can only be used
> if they are on hand when they're needed. ... Moreover, no vital
> era was ever engendered by a theory. It was first of all a game,
> a conflict, a journey.[20]

Architecture, Capitalism and the 'Autonomy' of the Political

David Cunningham

Let me start again with two passages from my interlocutors' texts. The first of these would be Erik's endorsement of a position, identified in his case with Alain Badiou and Jacques Rancière, for which, he argues, "the democratic political is not a reflection of something else, like the cultural, the social, or the economic," but instead must be "absolutely separated" from "socio-economic analysis" in order to think "the political' as its own "immanent field of action." The second comes from Libero's analysis of what he calls "the architecture of *autonomy*", as opposed to "the autonomy of *architecture*", which—particularly as it derives from Pier Vittorio Aureli's retrieval of Raniero Panzieri's and Mario Tronti's workerist *autonomia*, and what Libero calls its "hyper-politicized discourse"—would, he suggests, cut through the paralyses of "mediation and reflexivity" and demand "an explicit commitment to a project of political change", "placing a political program ahead of any market mechanism."

The references here are to two very different (even competing) traditions: Italian workerist-autonomist and French post-Althusserian, respectively. Yet, for all their manifest differences, and the very different visions of emancipation that animate them, one can perhaps recognize in these two citations two variants or echoes of a more familiar refrain going back not only to the 1960s but, indeed, to the first decades of the twentieth century and to the arguments of, variously, Gramsci, Luxemburg, Bernstein, and even Lenin. Battling against an "economic determinism", what comes to be at stake in each is a question of the "autonomy of the political" itself. Framed to this degree *against* a certain "Marxist tradition", as Aureli puts it, such arguments seek to identify, at their most emphatic, "not the degree of autonomy of one level from the other, but the autonomy of political power *tout court* with respect to economic determinations."[1]

If nothing else—and this is my difficulty—one finds raised in this a larger series of questions about "politics" and "the political" which would be fairly impossible to address in any adequate fashion in the space available to me here. Indeed, although Peggy, in particular, makes an admirable attempt in her contribution to stick close to questions concerning those practical possibilities available to the architect within the institutions within which she or he actually works, it is evident that in the pieces by Libero and, in particular, Erik, there is an inevitable—and by no means undesirable—tendency for "architectural" questions to give way to far more general issues of political strategy and theory, or, indeed, the nature of politics or the political per se.

Of course there are good reasons for this. In fact, one might even say that many of the arguments adduced here as countering Tafuri's position might actually be read, ironically, as offering rather strong support for them, insofar as one of his key claims in the conclusion to *Architecture and Utopia* is precisely that "[r]eflection on architecture, inasmuch as it is a criticism of the concrete 'realized' ideology of architecture itself, cannot but go beyond this and arrive at a specifically political dimension."[2] Indeed, for all our differences, this is one point that Erik and I can apparently agree on: the impossibility of treating architectural theory or practice in isolation from far wider questions concerning the existence or otherwise of "emancipatory political sequences" which can never be regarded as "architectural" in themselves. (Although no doubt my own position would remain, for Erik, far too tied to those forms of "real cynicism" that he imagines he locates, like so many others today, in "the negative dialectic of critique" *tout court*.) For better or worse, the result, at any rate, is that our discursive terrain shifts away from attention to any specific architectural practice as such, and instead towards the respective merits of, say, Badiou or Rancière, Negri or Tronti, as competing starting points for a contemporary political thought more generally—and so what follows will, hence, of necessity address the arguments of my interlocutors largely in such terms.

Before wondering what this might mean for architecture— certainly a central concern of Libero's text—we would need then to start with the question of what we are to make of contemporary arguments for the autonomy of politics or the political per se? In order to cut to the chase, let me say from the outset that the danger of naïveté is, I think, for me, that the gesture of separation between "the autonomy of political power" and "economic determinations" can very quickly become not merely an insistence on the autonomy of the political but on its *primacy*. Among other things—as with Laclau and Mouffe—this explains the otherwise inexplicable turn of a Leftist thinker like Tronti to the work of Carl Schmitt as a decisively non-Marxist resource for thinking a "politics" beyond "political economy."[3] The high price paid for this, however, is that an (entirely justifiable, if hardly new) critique of economic determinism can come, as it does in much post-Althusserian philosophy, to be equated with a straightforward elision of the very problem of "capitalism" altogether, which, it is worth reminding ourselves, can scarcely be thought *at all* without at least some attention to the power of the "economic" as regards the social forms and relations of modern societies. And, as Ellen Meiksins Wood puts it, "if our starting point is *capitalism*, then we need to know exactly what kind of starting point this is."[4]

To the degree, then, that the combination of "Karl und Carl" — which is, as Aureli recalls, one of the chapters of Tronti's *La politica al tramonto* — is not then simply to become Schmitt *as opposed to* Marx,[5] part of what is at stake must rather be a question of the degree to which it is possible to maintain the latter's own "lesson" that the very possibility of socialism or communism — communism as "the *real* movement of history" (a phrase I read quite differently from Erik) — rests on the capacity for such a "movement" to be found developing "internally" to the social forms of capitalist modernity itself, including those "instantiated" in a modern architecture. While this is certainly in accordance with Tronti's argument (indeed it is central to it), Rancière could, for example, hardly be more explicit in his rejection of such a position, making clear that, for him, "[u]nequal society does not carry any equal society in its womb", just as "capitalist forms of production and exchange" do not constitute "the material conditions for an egalitarian society."[6]

For Rancière, of course, this runs alongside a more general dismissal of "critical theory" that has, in this context, a somewhat enigmatic resonance with what (borrowing from the title of a 2007 collection) Libero terms the "new pragmatism" or "post-critical turn" in recent architectural thought. Certainly the latter would endorse Erik's definition of the "ultimate aim of politics" as one of changing "the given socio-environmental ordering in a certain manner...the architectural practice *par excellence*" (albeit to rather different ends). But if any such "intervention" is "a violent act [which] erases at least partially what is there in order to erect something new and different", it is hard to see — from either perspective — how this (and the "painstaking organization" that, as Erik rightly says, would have to accompany it) is actually aided by passing over a critical attempt to understand the solidity of "the given socio-environmental ordering" itself. This is not to say that new forms of collectivity (including those invoked by various modern architectural sequences) do not have to be constituted through both "positive" common action and what E.P. Thompson termed the building of "shared consciousness", to a degree that more dogmatically "critical" strands of Marxist theory have often underplayed. Nonetheless, such consciousness is still, at some level, a question of becoming conscious of what is an *objective* situation.[7] That "the democratic political" is not, in this sense, "a *reflection* of something else, like the cultural, the social, or the economic" does not mean that it can therefore be severed from them. The relationship between "creating" and "discovering" forms of collective identity is a good deal more complex and "dialectical."

By contrast, the Rancièrian critique of *any* notion of "scientific" understanding as a grounding for political practice—for fear of, in Erik's words, "situat[ing] the intellectual, Plato's philosopher-king, in the driver's seat of radical urban politics"—does not so much rework emancipatory politics as it risks simply dissolving it into sheer free-floating voluntarism and arbitrary ethical commitment, in which "politics" is imagined to be somehow free of all *social* mediation.[8] However, once this route is taken, the "autonomy of the political" risks becoming itself little more than an abstract and ungrounded plea for "a rebirth of the Idea" that proves unable to get beyond the interminable repetition of the abstract demand itself. Symptomatically, it is unsurprising that while, for example, Badiou's recent work is full of assertions of the need for new models of organization and political practice, he actually has almost nothing to say *about* these new forms beyond the continual indication of their necessity.

Not without some hesitancy, it is in this regard that I wonder, too, quite what to make of that "insurgent architecture" in which Erik asks us, once freed of critical inertia, to make our investment. For while there may be a number of gestures towards *where*, in general terms, new "experiment[s] with...the spatialized contours of more egalitarian forms of urban life" might be constructed in Erik's piece—the squares and plazas of recent insurrections, as well as the proliferating megalopolises of the global South—there is a notable lack of practical detail concerning of what such 'experiments' and "innovations" might actually consist. Despite, then, Erik's several references to "the vibrant insurgent architectural practices visible and lived in the interstitial spaces of imperial and cosmopolitan global urbanization", and "radical ega-libertarian political experimentations *already* present", his piece is strikingly thin as regards to any *specific* delineation of what these practices might actually be. Yet if it is true that no emancipatory politics can—outside of the chimera of communal immediacy or the eradication of representational forms *per se*—finally be separated off from the question of its institutions, then it is notable (and we should be frank about this) that, as one recent commentator has put it, in fact "precisely to the extent that current insurgencies *haven't*, except fugitively, given rise to new institutions, they have left the new life precisely as a matter of desire, which is to say of lack."[9] In the face of this, an admirable optimism of both will and intellect can easily float free of any "real movement" whatsoever.

These are practical and strategic points—and important as such—but they also, then, touch upon broader questions of the relationship between politics and economy (or, more properly, "political economy") under capitalism in general, as these might inflect a rather more complex sense of the relations between structure *and* agency than current philosophies of the autonomy of the political would seem to allow. Like Jameson, I am of the view that a good part of the fundamental *originality* of Marx's work—and what sets it apart from competing utopian socialist, anarchist or conspiratorial politics of the nineteenth century—*is* indeed its emphasis on the economic; not necessarily as an "economism" (through which all questions of politics might simply be *reduced* to "the economic base") but in the sense of insisting upon precisely the impossibility of thinking politics *autonomously* of the broader socio-economic forces and dynamics that make up capitalism as a system.[10] This is not necessarily to dispute the argument made by Poulantzas and others that classical Marxism lacked, in many respects, a fully-developed account of modern political institutions, and of the state in particular, but it is worth bearing in mind that more thorough-going attempts to shift the discourse in the direction of discussions of "power," "domination," or, even, "democracy"—attempts that have their principal origins in either revisionism or longer antagonisms with anarchist thought—can also obscure the emphasis on economic exploitation (as distinct from direct political oppression or hierarchy), as well as on those *social* relations of abstraction produced by the logics of commodification and the money form, that made the Marxian *critique* of political economy so powerful in the first place.[11] It is ironic from this perspective that the current resurgence in assertions of the autonomy of the political should take place at the very moment in which the "globalization" of capitalist modernity tends to reveal the ways in which economic "interests" precisely over-determine "political" forms and institutions to an unprecedentedly profound degree.

In this sense, to put it a little polemically, there is a danger that contemporary articulations of autonomy, in a very different context than that in which someone like Tronti wrote, tend either to fantasize the very real defeats of the twentieth century Left *as* some hidden victory—the "post-Fordist" destruction of the welfare state and extension of "real subsumption" in fact heralding the liberation of the autonomous creativity of the multitude—or to retreat into the promise of "rare" messianic incursions conveniently freed or extracted from the conditions of any socio-historical reality as such. More broadly, it is hard not to suspect that this very contemporary anxiety to assert the absolute autonomy of the political, far from reflecting some *actual* renewed strength of political militancy—one that often seeks signs of its "real" embodiment in a theoretical appropriation of the Arab Spring or Occupy—in fact reflects the very contemporary dominance *of* capital in the determination of social relations (including ones beyond "the market" narrowly conceived) and hence of "the economic" itself. Indeed, this would seem, slightly paradoxically, to be a good part of what simultaneous discussions around the "post-political" or "post-democracy", in the likes of Mouffe and Rancière, register (while being, almost constitutively, unable to "explain" them). But the problem here is not resolved simply by renewing our exhortations to "be political", or burdening actual movements of political resistance with unrealistic expectations, with the inevitable disappointment that follows from them, as if we could overcome the (structural) tendency of the hegemony of the value form to de-politicize the social relations of contemporary societies simply by idealistically willing capitalism away.

Much of what I am arguing here is hardly new of course. Indeed, Slavoj Žižek, who might otherwise be thought of as rather close to Badiou in questions of politics at least, makes a similar point, in which he argues that the "ultimate Marxian parallax" itself might be identified as one "between economy and politics, between the 'critique of political economy' with its logic of commodities and the political struggle with its logic of antagonism." From the perspective of such antinomies, what he calls the "pure politics" of a post-Althusserian discourse that would include Badiou and Rancière, as well as Laclau and Mouffe, tends then to seek "the reduction of the sphere of economy...to an 'ontic' sphere deprived of 'ontological' dignity."[12] Yet, it's unclear why one should have to accept as such Žižek's own suggestion that "the relationship between economy and politics" should thus be understood as akin to "that of the well-known visual paradox of the 'two faces or a vase': one either sees the two faces or a vase, never both of them," since the capacity to "see" the two together is surely the basis of a dialectical thought (such as Žižek has elsewhere been at pains to defend).[13] For what such positions fail to acknowledge is precisely the degree to which the value form is the dominant form of the *social* in contemporary capitalist societies. If Žižek does indeed recognize this, here at least, however, he concedes far too much to Badiou in suggesting that, as a result, the "economic" is somehow "irreducible to politics" "in its very form." For the fact that capital over-determines modern social relations, *including politics*—and this is, after all, what "capitalism" means—surely entails that we require new ways of thinking the relationship of an emancipatory politics *to* the forms of contemporary capitalism, rather than arguing that we need somehow to bracket off or maintain a principled indifference to capital in order to remain uncontaminated by it; a position that merely results in the revival of a *romantic* anti-capitalism.[14] Here, what was once, in the 1960s and '70s, a serious and necessary attempt to complicate an "orthodox" base-superstructure model that reduced questions of politics (or law or culture, and so on) to the economic—with all the problems of the notorious Althusserian debates around "*relative* autonomy" and "determination in the last instance"—becomes a simple evasion and effacement of questions of political economy altogether. At any rate, a mere *inversion* of the primacy of politics and economy—which merely swaps the "old" problems of seeking to explain all political phenomena as determined by either capital's reproduction requirements or "ruling class interests" for a determination of the entire social field by something called "the political"—is hardly a satisfactory solution.

This is not to deny that capitalism certainly requires "politics" to take root and reproduce itself, as we know from the work of Polanyi, among others, and as the emergence of neo-liberalism as a political project since the 1970s makes clear. But just as this does not mean that the State therefore can be entirely reduced to its contribution to such reproduction, as Poulantzas rightly objected, so, conversely, it does not mean that "the capitalist economy" (as itself a "social order") can be solely reduced to a question of its political formation. At the very least, this would leave us fundamentally unequipped to understand from where the apparently *de*-politicizing dynamics of capitalism are derived, given that, logically, these, too, must, according to such an account, be at some level politically constituted. In fact, as Susan Buck-Morss points out, insofar as it produces a kind of "collectivity" quite different from that of the *polis* or older model of "the people," "the *depersonalization* of economic exchange within capitalist society", which is *intrinsic* to the money form, also "depoliticizes economic power, *no matter* how close capitalists and politicians may become."[15] From this perspective, "neo-liberalism" — much as it requires the political power of states and state-like institutions to effect its transformations — simply intensifies, and reconstitutes in new ways, capitalism's own *self-defining* separation of the political from the economic, whereby issues of democratic equality or representation are safely isolated from issues of economic equality, exploitation and social power.

If nothing else, this should then make us wary, I think, of for example Aureli's attempt, in some of his writings published since *The Project of Autonomy*, to define — following Chantal Mouffe's own Schmittian account — the "sphere of the political" as that "sphere in which a part, a group of individuals, acquires knowledge of itself in the form of knowing what it is, what it ought to be, what it wants, and what it does now want", as if such a "sphere" could be thought entirely *abstracted* from the social relations of political economy as such. If this provides the basis, for Aureli, of equating the political with the dimension of the "formal" in architecture, whereby politics as "agonism through separation and confrontation" can be placed alongside "the process of separation inherent in the making of architectural form", there is something profoundly *formalist* about this definition of "the sphere of the political" itself, which in rendering "separation and confrontation" solely internal to politics, merely brackets off the central "context" of actual, historical capitalist social relations themselves.[16]

Similarly, what might be thought of as a justifiable fear of foreclosing upon "the openness and contingency" of politics can easily slip into simple evasion of the question of how capitalist institutions continue (at an increasingly planetary level) to transform and reproduce themselves. In this way, the voluntarist emphasis on a necessity of contingency risks becoming the pretext for a failure to engage *all* questions of what Sartre called the "practico-inert" or the relative durability and stability of specific crystallizations of existing social relations (including those constitutive of architecture as institution and ideology). While it may be the case, as Erik puts it, that the political is "always disruptive", emerging through "the refusal to observe the 'place' allocated to people and things", without some notion of *re*-allocation, and how it is to be organized and sustained, it is impossible to ever get beyond the (occasional and temporary) *moment* of "disruption" itself. This is particularly unfortunate in the context of the current discussion, since it is also most clearly where questions of the built environment and infrastructure—as, at some level, material instantiations of a certain socio-economic "practico-inert"—become of paramount importance, even if these are far from reducible to "architectural" questions in any narrow disciplinary sense.

Architecture and Politics Again

Aureli's account of an "architecture of autonomy" rests on an affirmation of architecture's capacity for both a *resistant* and *productive* autonomy from the dominant socio-spatial dynamics of the metropolis, which, at the same time, presents a kind of "symbolic" power manifested in the urban fragment to imply the ways in which a socialist city might arise "within but against the forms of the bourgeois city." Although its philosophical and political lineage may then seem quite different, in several respects this repeats the broad strategy embedded in that kind of "counter-hegemonic" enclave that Jameson, in his famous 1982 reading of Tafuri, locates in the very "'Utopianism' of the modern movement in architecture" itself, for which "new and still nascent social relations [of the socialist city] ... [are] theorized in terms of small yet strategic pockets or beachheads within the older system [the bourgeois city]": "laboratories in which original social relations of the future are being worked out."[17] To the degree that this might be understood as itself a potential manifestation of *political* autonomy, particularly among the early avant-gardes, this might then conjoin, in turn, with a certain strong political reading of Gramscian hegemony itself.[18]

Significantly, too, of course, it is the status of such counter-hegemony, precisely as an autonomously *political* project, that is similarly at stake in the dispute between Tafuri and Tronti in their respective analyses of Red Vienna, in what is, in many ways, the center piece of Aureli's book[19]—a dispute we presumably don't need to run through again. No doubt Tafuri's judgement here is too absolute, too austere in its (retrospective) presentation of the seemingly *total* "failure" of such projects, where Red Vienna or (slightly less damningly) the German social democratic *Siedlungen* are concerned.[20] Still, it is worth asking: who exactly could deny that these *were* failures judged by their own criteria (or that Rossi's exercises in "autonomy" have fared any better)? Moreover, the "lesson" of the limits of autonomy in the face of the dominance of *capitalist* social and spatial relations remains, I think, pretty apposite today; however "cynical" such a "realist" judgement may be. From this perspective, anyway, while it may be true, as Aureli writes, that "Rossi's autonomy of architecture was above all about the establishment of urban concepts that posited the supremacy of politics over the city's accelerating economic development," they surely give us an actual lesson, historically, in the precise opposite—namely, if anything, the *supremacy* of "the city's accelerating economic development" over any autonomous "politics"; a lesson that, despite its "cynicism," I'm not sure we can afford to ignore today.[21]

At the same time, it is far from clear to me that Aureli's conception of an architecture of autonomy can be separated from what are, after all, the very *historically-specific* arguments made by Tronti for remaining within the Italian Communist Party in the context of a series of political debates that are hardly our own. The attempt in Aureli to mobilize these arguments in order to damn the supposed "liberal" postmodernism of Negri and others at the beginning of the twenty-first century can, as a result, appear more than a little surreally disconnected from contemporary political and socio-economic realities, given that the option of working within any kind of equivalent to the Party—and the kind of counter-hegemonic project that this envisaged—can hardly appear as a viable option today. More generally, one might wonder just how far the return to Italian debates of the 1960s and 1970s is really going to aid the kinds of "re-politicization of architecture", as Libero puts it, "that was a central feature of Modern Architecture from the start" *now*, particularly given that these largely precede that neo-liberal "revolution in reverse" which he rightly presents as a necessary "political context" in which to think about the possibilities of contemporary architecture in general.

Perhaps this is to be related, too—by contrast to Badiou's or Rancière's (or Negri's) principled "distance from the State"—to

Aureli's own reminder that Tronti's "reflections on the autonomy of the political" turned increasingly from the end of the 1960s towards an "approach" directed at "the level of State institutions" themselves, "posing a Marxist-Communist 'counterplan' to the one of liberal capitalism."[22] However, such properly socialist "goals" also surely take us back to the very same problems with which we began, and raise the same kinds of questions about what this would mean today. Libero stresses the necessity of any "architecture of autonomy" working to "develop to the fullest possible extent a politicized theory and practice of design" that might contribute to "the reversal of neo-liberalism as its most immediate political goal." As he continues: "Such a prospect would mean, for starters, massive public investments in housing, infrastructure, health, education and welfare programs ... The size of such investments would have to be at least as great as those employed to resuscitate the financial industry—short of which, as David Harvey notes, no real alternative to the neo-liberal city is possible." Yet how can any autonomy of *design* plausibly define its *own* goals at such a "scale" ("equal or greater" Libero suggests than that required by "Reaganism"), at least without its mediation by similarly larger social forces and institutions? The Rossian urban "fragments" celebrated by Aureli certainly seem to have little purchase here. Indeed, in this respect, if not in others, we seem rather closer to Tafuri's critical reservations about the practical possibilities of the "enclave" than to Aureli's affirmation of an architecture of autonomy. "[M]assive public investments in housing, infrastructure, health, education and welfare programs" are very evidently not a purely "political goal" that can be realized (or perhaps even envisioned as such) by a "theory and practice of design", however "politicized"; not least because this involves some fairly obvious "economic" questions. (What, for example, would be the role of money itself in such "investment"?)

This is perhaps why—unless I am profoundly misreading

him—I'm also slightly bewildered by Libero's assertion that the possibility of some autonomist-style "movement" of "re-politicization" has its "most obvious precedent" in "the vast building programs that were realized ... in the aftermaths of the two World Wars, the Russian Revolution, and the Great Depression," the remains of which, he continues, "still make up a good part of the urban fabric of cities from Paris to Vienna to Amsterdam and New York." For if this is the "precedent," what "building programs" exactly are these a precedent of? In fact, the obvious conclusion is that it is precisely the *absence* of such programs that attests to the absence—outside of Latin America at least—of those "socialist administrations" (or, at any rate, broadly social democratic ones) that, as Libero notes, actually made possible such programs in the first place. (Given the influence of Latin American "new socialism" as well as of a certain conception of the autonomy of the political drawn from Laclau's populism, this might be the place to insert a discussion of the recent advances of new European political parties like Syriza and Podemos—both as regards the difficult, properly strategic questions regarding their capacity to maintain a certain democratic "autonomy" in the face of European and global financial and intra-state institutions, and their attempt to mobilize and *institutionalize* the more purely "insurrectional" politics of the square and *indignados*.)

Recent history would seem, at any rate, to fatally complicate the autonomist story of capitalist development, as Tronti himself seems to have come to realize, since, even if the (now waning) gains of the twentieth century registered in the welfare state or Keynesian "fixes," do indeed reflect both a reshaping of capitalism by workers' struggles, and, as Aureli argues, the extent to which "capitalism was forced to take the initiative politically and act with a certain independence from the economic determinants of its policies,"[23] it is far less plausible to see this as being the case when it comes to neo-liberalism (at least without somehow presenting the dismantling of the welfare state as a *victory* for the multitude; as, indeed, Negri effectively does). Yet this then poses a problem for Aureli too, since, arguably, the very "autonomy" available to Tronti (or Rossi), in both the political and architectural institutions of their time, rested, in a sense, on a platform built by what Libero calls the "left hand" of the state's "social programs" that are now in the process of being dismantled. Indeed, as the urban theorist Margit Mayer points out, "even if this was not widely admitted by the activist benefi-ciaries", it was, in fact, often the very "Keynesian-welfarist and social-collectivist institutions" which "earlier provided a material basis for much of the progressive movement activity" that precisely celebrated self-organization and its own autonomy.[24]

Beyond the Polis

Let me conclude by turning to one of the two epigraphs to Erik's piece, which he takes from Giorgio Agamben: "There is a shift from the model of the *polis* founded on a centre, that is, a public centre, or *agora*, to a new metropolitan spatialization that is certainly invested in a process of *de-politicization*." Now, there is evidently much truth in this. However, it is a truth that precisely *requires* us to grasp the ways in which it is the metropolis's "domination" by the money form, as Simmel described it back in 1903, that determines such apparent "de-politicization" itself, without which the very notion of the political that is being mobilized here recedes into mere archaism. For, even leaving aside all those well-known restrictions on the membership of the actual ancient *polis*, and of its "universalizing" democratic form, one can only begin, as Brecht would have put it, not from the "good old things" but from the "bad new ones."

In fact, as I have argued elsewhere—although I cannot elaborate the argument in the space available to me here—it is precisely a recognition of its *distance* from the urban form of the city as *polis* that is, it seems to me, the condition of any adequate theoretical engagement with urban politics today.[25] It is frustrating, then, that where Erik, for example, suggests that the "practices and experiments" necessitated by the "precarious" existence of the world's "slum dwellers" should "call for an urgent reconsideration of both urban theory and architectural praxis"—something upon which we can certainly agree—what such a "reconsideration" seems to amount to is a *return*, by way of Badiou's and Rancière's effectively trans-historical conception of the "political" itself, to "what the polis has always been."

Libero has good reason to wield his bat against Massimo Cacciari given the revelations about his subsequent political career detailed in Raffaele Liucci's (admirably muck-raking) *Il Politico della Domenica.* Nonetheless, whatever the limitations or problems of his "nihilistic version of workerism," which I certainly feel no compulsion to defend, there is at least one aspect of his "radical realism" that seems worth disinterring here: namely, his insistence on the historical breach constituted, politically as well as socially, by the form of the *metropolis* itself, as what he describes as the socio-spatial formation of "those differences that, as the measure and calculation of value, integrate *every phenomenon* into the dialectic of *abstract* value," and in which each particular "place" is rendered *equi-valent* in a universal circulation and exchange. This is certainly "economic" in form, but it is also profoundly *social* in the very fullest sense. As Cacciari thus rightly implies, drawing here on Simmel's famous essay, far from being a simple continuation of the "city" or *polis*, the metropolis emerges, on the contrary, as the manifestation of a distinctively modern productive logic of *abstraction* which opposes and unsettles it: "an uprooting from the limits of the *urbs*, from the social circles dominant within it, from its *form*."[26]

It is this, I think, that throws a different light on Erik's citation of Neil Brenner's recent work on "planetary urbanization' and his call for a "revised theorization that is adequate to the contemporary urban condition." (Of course, if politics *is* to be absolutely separated from "socio-economic analysis," as Rancière suggests, one might wonder why understanding and responding to planetary urbanization's "supplant[ing of] older forms of the urban" is something we actually need to take account of, or indeed be adequate to, at all …). For if Erik is rightly critical of a "politics articulated around a localized *ethos* rather than an infinitely inclusive *demos*," it is hard to see how, in such a context, a simple *scaling up* of the "political" form of the polis or agora as "space of encounter" can really be adequate to the difficulties thereby posed; not least as regards the forms of social abstraction and mediation that this would inevitably require. (Practically speaking, of course, this is one problem faced by the move from the "urban rebellion" as sited in the "public" square, where "a new sensibility about the polis" might seem more plausible, to the wider social space of the metropolis surrounding it.) Indeed, this is part of the wider importance of what Peggy—following her citation of Erik Olin Wright's plea to think through "what it means to struggle positively for socialism rather than simply against capitalism"—observes, via David Harvey, as capitalism's success in "constructing the institutions that mediate, necessarily, between particulars (individual aspirations) and universals (agreed upon rights)." As Peggy continues, "any radical politics" no doubt has to find ways of mediating between particular and universal in similarly plausible and "appealing" ways. To put it bluntly then, on a planet "housing" seven billion people, forms of mediation, abstraction and impersonality are not only ineliminable but *necessary* to the construction of new social relations and modes of collective transformation of our increasingly urbanized world. Unmoored from its historically specific conditions or mode of production, returns to the *polis* offer little here, and, at worse, serve only to render our "alienation" interminable.

The point is then not to put the political back in its place, securely subordinated to the economic, but, first, to forestall naïveté about what politics "alone" could really be in our contemporary extension of a "metropolitan spatialisation", and the new forms of social relationality accompanying it, towards a planetary urbanization, and, second, to wonder how, if "politics" and "political economy" *are* to be thought together, we might better understand what we might mean by "revolution" itself today. As I suggested in my first piece, a start at least might be made by recognizing that no revolution is ever *purely* political (this is the disastrous starting point of current enthusiasms for some metaphysics of *the* Event and of the absolute separation of "truth" and "knowledge"), but is always also *social* in a far wider sense — part of what Jameson terms "the whole lengthy, complex, contradictory process of systemic transformation."[27] But this also entails a coming to terms with the ineliminability of abstraction itself as a central dimension of all modern societies, beyond all the temptations of nostalgia for the mythical communal immediacy of encounter projected back into the *polis* as an urban-social form. For is it in fact possible to imagine some form of urban connectivity or "commons" that would *not* involve fundamental forms of abstraction and mediation? Certainly, as far as any plausible contemporary *metropolitan* politics of emancipation and transformation is concerned, it is here that architecture plays its own messy, complex, contradictory role today.

7

Architecture/Agency/Emancipation

Peggy Deamer

The papers of my colleagues Erik, David, and Libero responding to the questions we exchanged have yielded stimulating if particular positions. The stakes are high for all of us, given our respect for each other and our interest in establishing our own claim to radicality and the emancipatory project. In this array of thoughtful provocations, though, identical terms are deployed so differently that their meanings slip around. Those differences, we might say, make evident the cause of frustration with the state of theory today; this is probably why Lahiji had us do what we are doing.

There are two terms in particular that are worth parsing out in order to establish not what we do and do not agree on but what constitutes the larger epistemological framework within which our different opinions operate. These two words are "architect" and "autonomy". A look at how these two terms are understood allows me to initiate a theory of emancipatory architecture.

Architect

As suggested by my own response to the questions put forth by my colleagues, I am curious about how "architect"—as a term and as a certain type of individual—folds into "architecture". Erik and I agree, I believe, that the term "architecture" (as a discipline, profession, or cultural symbol) in the emancipatory context is conceptually distracting. Erik is very clear in his (I think smart) identification that while architecture is what Tafuri claimed it to be—ideology's pawn—architects are not. My paper makes clear my impatience with the abstraction of "architecture" as the

supposed object of our theoretical missive. I would say, "architecture" is useful only when differentiating from other disciplines, not as an entity with agency. Libero and David, on the
other hand, have faith in "architecture" to hear our calling and to
adjust in the direction of emancipation.

But there are still differences within these pairings. Erik,
unlike me, is primarily concerned with the distinction between
the radical architect and the insurgent architect. His distinction,
based on Harvey's "insurgent architect," claims that only the
insurgent architect has the right to "emancipatory" claims. Mere
"radical" architects make gestures and posture, but in Erik's
account, effective agency rests solely with the insurgent
architect. Regardless of ones agreement or not with this
judgement, there is both a narrowing and a broadening of the
term "architect": narrowing for the insurgent being a small
subset of architects; broadening for its seeing the architect more
as a generalized, if political and theoretically adept, citizen than
a trained professional.

For me, the "architect" is a constructed subject, trained in
specific ways. Those ways include the reading of theory, the
looking at images, the designing of buildings, the participation
in accredited schools of architecture and, maybe even, subjecting
oneself to the regime of licensure. When we address the
"architect" in the context of the emancipatory project, I'm interested in anyone of those who might think past a client-driven
practice and put their spatial expertise toward thwarting private
development. I sense that I feel more strongly than the others
that the specific way that architects are trained—school,
licensure, professional identification—is central, not peripheral,
to the emancipatory project or its current lack there of. The
others do mention the need for discovering alternative modes of
practice but glance off the particulars. We might call mine a
particularly narrow definition of the term "architect", but
narrowness is meant to identify the center around which the

periphery—"architecture"—is organized.

Libero and David for their shared embrace of "architecture", understand the term differently. Libero sees "architecture" as artifacts (spaces or buildings) that have the ability to teach society emancipatory behavior. It takes a smart architect to produce such an artifact, but that artifact ("architecture") is the agent of change. The theorist might address the designer/architect/builder/maker to motivate him or her politically and aesthetically, but it is the product/artifact/architecture operating subliminally on the user's/consumer's psyche that matters. This concern for the product puts his analysis in the realm of cultural consumption—how is the artifact communicating and categorizing; how is it appropriated—while Erik's and mine rests in the realm of cultural (and actual) production. The ultimate audience of theory is not the architect, but the user of her artifacts.

David is more concerned with architecture as a discipline than as an object (spatial or material, urban or building) or object producer. How has the discipline been circumscribed? What is at stake in the "building"/"architecture" dichotomy? What tasks has capitalist development taken away form "architecture"? Not all of this ignores the efficacy of the object—he clearly wants urban spaces that do emancipatory work—and there are conscious conflations between "architecture" and "architects"— in discussing Zaera-Polo, he registers the "agency of architecture" with the "authorial architect"; he studies various "concepts of architecture and, crucially, of 'the architect'"—but he clearly analyzes "architecture" as a disciplinary subset of capitalism, one that has, as he answers his own questions about what it has surrendered in this context, given away too much.

Ultimately, his is a historical project, not an ontological one, with architecture at the center—ala Habermas in his defense of the modern project over Lyotard's of postmodernism—of a yet to be fulfilled modern project. In this, there is sympathy with

Libero. But the conflation of architecture and buildings shows a greater difference between Libero and David than is immediately apparent. The successful realization of "architecture" for David would leave behind the aesthetic distinction between building and architecture while Libero, I believe, holds fast to that difference. Libero has optimism about architecture escaping capitalism's grip if only one can get the "architecture of autonomy" right; David doesn't, but still wants to do better within a suspension of disbelief.

My sense of the implications of these different approaches to agency embedded in the "architect"/"architecture" definition will be parsed out more completely as we examine autonomy— intimately linked to ones position on the potential agency of "architecture". But the divisions here indicate the ambivalence critical theory has on who or what its audience is.

Autonomy

As suggested, "architecture" and "autonomy" are linked; there is a correlation between enthusiasm for the autonomy and for architecture as an entity. If you believe in "architecture" as a stable subject/entity, you (can) believe in its autonomy. Thus Libero and David pick up the autonomy issue directly and Erik and I do not. Or, to be more accurate, while we all clearly believe that architecture as a discipline does particular special things that no other discipline does, Libero and David explore its conceptual advantages. But there is a difference in what "autonomy" implies for David and Libero and, I suggest, for Erik and I (even as we are silent about it).

Libero's view of autonomy is more positively layered than David's. In faulting K. Michael Hays (whose view of autonomy is too aesthetic and too stripped of politics) for assuming autonomy as a "fact" and not a "value," he contradicts David's belief that it is a fact: autonomy as he says is not something you can be for or against, it just is. But pointing to this difference (that does have ideological implications) should not misdirect us from the more operative distinction regarding aesthetics. While Libero wants a non-aesthetic approach to autonomy, embedded in his desire for an "architecture of autonomy" instead of an "autonomy of architecture"; aesthetics is still architecture's disciplinary framework. His appeal to Adorno—which, despite Libero's plea that Adorno not be used in the de-politicized mode of K. Michael Hays and the Anglo-Saxon tradition—supports design's capacity to transcend capitalist hegemony. As we know, Adorno's 1938 essay, "On the Fetish Character in Music and the Regression of Listening"—an essay in which Adorno dismisses Walter Benjamin's "The Work of Art in the Age of Mechanical Reproduction" as crude Marxism for its concern for the labor of aesthetic production—celebrates aesthetic/design transcendence. His definition of what a successful utopian project would entail— "an exploration through *architectural*, (emphasis his) as well as political means", "in which aesthetic *and* (emphasis his) the political are inseparable, co-extensive dimensions of design"— makes his position clear.

A non-aesthetic approach to design, then, assumes a much broader definition of "design" than we have traditionally understood. Indeed, Libero indicates it should embrace "legal, political, and financial" matters and the attention to "cooperative arrangements like community development corporations and land trusts." This seems legitimate if hard to imagine in an aesthetic context. But the larger question is whether to accommodate a non-aesthetic approach to autonomy (the term "autonomy" is so stretched that it loses it conceptual value), a question made easier to answer in the affirmative when the example of the "the architecture of autonomy" fails to deliver, for Libero or the reader. For Libero, his favored project—Pier Vittorio Aureli's *Rome: the Center(s) Elsewhere?*—is conceptually right but aesthetically wrong. For us, the supposed aesthetic failure of the project indicates its conceptual impossibility.

What Libero really argues for in his defense of autonomy is its resistance to "the grand narrative of US corporate architecture," "degraded professionalism," and "the dominant business model of the profession." This raises some conundrums—aren't legal, political, and financial matters part of the "business" question? But it indicates an enemy that we can all agree on, even if some of us think autonomy is the best way to attack it.

David, as indicated in the "architecture" discussion, evokes autonomy less as a condition of design and more as a structural condition of capitalism. You do not, again, choose to be for it or against it. Despite the fact that he, too, evokes Adorno—in this case, for pointing out (I love this) that architecture necessarily operates in a society it didn't produce—David, I believe, applies an Althusserian approach to "autonomy". Architecture is understood as a particular discipline that, like any other, is unique in its capitalist negotiations. Yes, David suggests (interestingly I think) that "architecture is a privileged site for understanding the changing character of 'intellectual labor' in capitalist development" (the site, by the way, that Libero implicates in the autonomy discussion by reference to *autonomia* but does not pursue) but that privilege is not linked to cultural hegemony. Likewise, David's "autonomy is not something you are for or against, but a reality in which architecture is enmeshed" shows that advocating for emancipatory architecture is not *via* a discourse on autonomy; it's *within* the discourse of autonomy.

A revealing indication of what is at stake for David in his analysis of autonomy is the implied (if I have this right, for there is ambiguity about his fascination with this; one gets it more from knowing his work) belief that architecture should not be so concerned with distinguishing itself from mere buildings. His emphasis on urbanism and urban planning comes with a desire to bypass this (to him) distinction, about which architects and architecture obsess but which, in the larger scheme of things, matters little to how our cities produce citizenship. There is much to be admired here, but in the context of emancipatory practices, its proper questioning of architecture's self-aggrandizement should not be equated with questioning the distinction between architects and builders, which I think he does. The first operates at the level of historical distance—one that, like Tafuri, suggests that architecture doesn't recognize its own pawned role in capitalism; the other operates at the level of professional construction over which we have control. To reiterate: one can and should agree with the thrust of David's desire to excise architecture's hubris as well as his obvious desire to move the discourse beyond architecture's objects without agreeing with the determinist framework in which it is found.

Erik's and my dismissal of autonomy (I brought up the validity of autonomy in an emancipatory architecture in the initial set of questions because I assumed we all thought "no" [1]) is linked by a commitment to the architect as agent of change and, I assume, a shared impatience with the indulgence given the autonomy discourse. But here, too, the dismissal is motivated by different "others" we would put in its place. As outlined in the "architect" discussion, he would put only "insurgent architects" there; I would put everyone initiated into the protocols of the discipline, especially those not yet indoctrinated in the old ways.

But Erik and David have forced me to think about what would be lost if we didn't appreciate architecture's unique disciplinary boundaries; its own special history and its own crazy infatuation with its formal prowess. If one embraces autonomy as a relative condition, there are insights to be gained. Historically, one can understand—in a manner reminiscent of Peter Burger's discourse on autonomy in his *Theory of the Avant Garde* but applied to architecture (not art) and addressing a different era (not the 30s but the 60s)—the attention paid to architectural/aesthetic autonomy as a necessary phase in architectural discourse. The 60s saw architecture being absorbed into the social sciences ("relevance;"

quantitative responses to aesthetics; community design that expunged the expertise of the architect; the Jane Jacobs effect) and the natural sciences (environmentalism, ecology). Architectural autonomy was a necessary response to save the discipline from non-creative forces. (Libero refers to this with good insights.) In the form of an Italian Tafuri/Rossi exposure of architecture's limits or in the form of American Eisenmanesque formalism—both similar in their intellectually rarefied arena— the autonomy discourse reclaimed architects' expertise and aesthetic criticality. From that original, stark delineation of autonomy, one can depict a move toward relativity has been on a steady march. Social autonomy[2] has increasingly infiltrated aesthetic autonomy, lessening the object aggrandizement and formal heroicism and replacing it with structures of social resistance. The move from an Eisenmanian formalism to the more nuanced one espoused by K. Michael Hays—for whom Mies van der Rohe offers "an object intractable to decoding by an analysis of what is only immanent and apparent"—is now followed by Pier Vittorio Aureli (and Libero's championing of him)—for whom architectural autonomy aligns with creative class labor. This historical move from absolute formal autonomy to increasingly social and relational autonomy is aided by thinkers such as Jacques Rancière, who avoids the division of the aesthetic and the social by positing an "aesthetic regime" found not in the art object but in the "sensorium of experience" shared by a set of potential citizens, and Maurizio Lazzarato—whose notion of "radical autonomy" insists that the identity of the worker, infused with affective, collective, and aesthetic intelligence, precedes capitalism.

Or, moving beyond this historical justification for indulging autonomy, one can investigate relative autonomy epistemologically, as a fundamental condition of how one thinks the discipline. One version of this—the purely aesthetic—would suggest that there is a stable language of architecture that responds within identifiable limits to changes in taste (which may or may not be related to social disruption). The representative versions of this would be Heinrich Wolfflïn who contrasted the formal parameters circumscribing the shift from Renaissance to Baroque architecture, or Wilhelm Worringer who saw changes of style within the boundaries of "abstraction" and "empathy." [3] Relative autonomy here is "relative" to changing cultural and aesthetic paradigms (changes in "style"), but the frame of that change is aesthetic.

The other more interesting version of this epistemological justification, though, is ideological. Max Weber posits the link between disciplinary autonomy and capitalism by identifying the necessary role that legislative autonomy (the discipline of law) played for capitalism to flourish; the independence of the legal system from the vagaries of the market offered an intellectual and structural rationality necessary for capitalism to be codifiable. Althusser likewise understands society as a complex structural whole with several relatively autonomous regions playing into that whole and conditioning one another. Althusser's "superstructure" is made up of both *repressive* state apparatuses (police, courts, prisons, armies) and *ideological* state apparatuses that work by persuasion, itself linked to its autonomy (that makes them look both inevitable and cool). Althusser identifies "interpellation" as the "hailing" of the subject into a position, an identity-forming misrecognition. To me, the system of relationships tying substrata to capitalism is constant (ideological) even as the particulars of how this is enacted in each discipline responds to historical necessity. I agree with David here.

In the post-Althusserian era, this understanding of the relative autonomy of disciplines has yielded two different implications. The first suggests that the fragmentation into the subsystems work only in one direction; once divided, each recursively produces their own elements from their own network of elements. This version is more depressing for the inability of these fragments to comment on the whole. My reading of David's support of Tafuri's "To search for an alternative within the structures that condition the very character of architectural design is indeed an obvious contradiction in terms" is agreement with this inevitability, even as I also read him as not abandoning the value, within this, of making more responsible urban spaces. ("I'm not sure that we can do without some measure of 'disenchanted' confrontation with the realties of the conditions and relations of production in which architecture must operate if we're to get anywhere in thinking about its possibilities and limits today.") The second suggests that each subsystem generates groups capable of experiencing the world and articulating their aspirations.[4] This is where I land: the subsystem has the capacity to address and irritate the larger system. If we don't, there is no one to blame but ourselves.

Theory of an Architecture of Emancipation

My position, already stated in my last paper, is that we too often collapse the idea of emancipation with the kinds of spaces we architects deliver: public? economically accessible to all members of society? programmatically democratic? — as opposed to how we understand and organize ourselves as producers of these spaces. There is a not so implicit suggestion on all the other authors' part that what is really meant by emancipatory architecture is public housing. This seems entirely too specific and mixes evidence with action.[5] My hope for a non-programmatically defined renewal of architectural production partially argues for "modeling" a better subsystem for society as a whole (some, like Donald Schön, the business management theorist of the 70s, believed that architecture, with its open and creative approach to work, is an ideal model for other subsystems [6]; David, with his "architecture is a privileged site for understanding the changing character of 'intellectual labor'" might also). But it mainly questions how we can presume to offer successful spatial gifts to society when we do not recognize our shared identity (as citizens/workers) with those who would build them or benefit from them. How we can recognize what constitutes "emancipatory" if we've never experienced in our own work/lives. How can a flawed institution based on sexism, racism, and hierarchical social status expect even to conceive of let alone produce liberating spaces?

I see the issue brought up by the "architect" and "autonomy" discussion through this lens. Hence my beef with Libero, whose anti-development sentiment I share but whose interest in "the architecture of autonomy" I do not. I neither believe it nor think it is the essential issue. Implicit in this is my siding, in the argument between Adorno and Benjamin regarding whether what we artist produce matters most (Adorno; the work of art must avoid easy consumption) or whether the means by which it is produced matters most (mechanical reproduction), with Benjamin.

If we take seriously the idea that we architects need to tidy up our own house (the discipline of architecture) before we can tidy up others, we need to establish who "architects" are; who is in and who is out of this discourse? Who, as Althusser would say, is being "called"? In what amounts to an institutional, class, and identity question, the work of Michel Foucault on disciplinary control and subject formation cannot be overlooked. If Althusser asks how a discipline interpellates the subjects it addresses, Foucault asks how it constitutes the rights and duties determining subjects and their relationships within and outside the discipline.[7] The identity of the architect should be viewed through the layers of disciplinary constructs.

Institutionally, we can distinguish between the discipline and the profession, the discipline encompassing academia. As indicated in my prior piece, I have faith in our ability to reshape what and how we teach architecture. There is much to say about the new topics, structures, and methods of research in contemporary architectural education—BIM,[8] ecology, inter-discipli-narity, entrepreneurialism—that indicate a move away from the nineteenth century-inspired Beaux-Arts system of architectural education. I have written about this elsewhere. But a source of this optimism is the example of geography, which, as a disci-pline, (it seems from the distance) has since the 70s redefined itself almost completely. Marxist geographers might technically be a subset of the discipline, but it seems that one cannot find an academic geographer who is NOT Marxists or neo-Marxists. One cannot account for this in terms of disciplinary content or dismiss this alliance as exceptional for its "natural" affinity to social amelioration. Certainly architecture has a greater calling in this regard. To this extent, I am less interested in Erik's use of David Harvey than how it is that Harvey redefined the subject in order to get the hearing and produce the students that he and the discipline do.

The rules that govern "professional" architecture education (in the US, NAAB), professional licensure (in the US, NCARB), and professional accolades (in the US, the AIA) are central to the definition of the "architect", both technically (you cannot call yourself an architect without licensure) and conceptually. AIA contracts keep architects separated from contractors and fabri-cators who are geared toward object, not knowledge delivery. AIA dues go to secure more government contracts and establish awards, foregoing any attempt to secure or reward socially responsible work or legal (let alone moral) labor practices. School accreditation mimics these protocols but also adds its own layer of misdirection by a culture of all-nighters and studio heroicism rewarding only flashy design. These regulations need to be done away with, ideally by de-professionalization. But the fact that they are all so dysfunctional does not mean that the training specific to a spatial practice be done away with.

The variously layered class issues embedded in the above constructs require untangling. As Althusser points out, each autonomous apparatus sets up its own social relations with its sites of class struggle. As a largely white-collar class, we identify with our private clients despite the fact that they are largely upper middle class to our marginally middle-middle class. We make sure we drive the same cars, drink the same wine, go to the same benefits because success likes to hire success and we architects are loath to admit that we are no longer a member of the (same) "gentleman's" class. In relation to public work, we see ourselves as trained experts that put our community clients on the other side of an education gap. In relationship to the contractors, we are white collar to their blue. In relationship to our bosses, we are workers to their managers.[9] These are not new points, but their listing in one place points to their inconsistency both with each other and with reality. And either because of or despite this, we turn our backs on a class discussion, supported in this denial by neo-liberalism having made "class" politics look old-school. Even if "class" is no longer defined exclusively by income and functions more clandestinely in ideology, the discussion needs to happen. Without it, we miss the opportunity to form allegiances that can push for change.

What then really is an architect, beyond its narrow professional designation? What kind of work do we do? Who do we identify with? Are we designers? makers? intellectuals? organizers? Despite my suggesting in the last paper that the optimism of Hardt, Negri, and Lazzarato has proved to be naïve as creative work turns into constant (and often unpaid) work, the discourse opened by immaterial labor still offers the best guide to better conceptualizations of the work of the architect. This suggests a number of things.

First, it identifies us with the Italian Operaism/worker movement, thereby reminding us that we are people first and workers second. While this humanist stance is in contradiction to Althusser's anti-humanism—and for that matter Foucault's biopolitics—it gives agency and empowerment within their determinism that allows us to not succumb without a fight. Second, we aren't makers. We don't deliver objects; we deliver spatial and organizational knowledge. We have expertise about precedent, publicness, urbanism, codes, aesthetics, citizenship, ecology, material behavior, human behavior, performance, spatial distribution, procurement, labor and environmental management.[10] Delivering objects consigns us to being piece-workers, both a conceptual problem (a missing object here or there doesn't trouble society) and an economic problem (the most abused form of compensation).[11] The corollary to this is that architects are intellectuals. As Pier Vittorio Aureli has pointed out, Tafuri's link to Operaism committed him to the idea of intellectual as a *worker*. His understanding of aesthetics "as a way to trust artworks not only as author's products but also as artefacts that revealed in their concreteness of object the sensual features of capitalist integration" was a radical rethinking of "the role of the architect and the planner as intellectual *worker*. This meant to shift the critique of ideology from the level of the architectural and urban project, to the form of intellectual work."[12] While this is (normally) associated with Tafuri's disparagement of design work altogether, its more effective thrust is the necessary infusion of intelligence in the architectural act.

I know this disagrees with Libero's dismissal of *autonomia* as an historical symptom of neo-liberalism rather than its proper critique. I disagree with this, or fail to see that they are different. But more essential is breaking down the distinction between manual and mental labor. Despite what this might look like, I *am* for that! I feel the most important message to architects (as immaterial workers) is that we ARE workers. If we are different than makers, we are not better than makers. The way to get architects to agree that there is no division between manual and mental work is to convince them first that they are workers at all. We have to give architects a description that is recognizable *and* transformable. Linked to my appreciation of David's suggestion that "architecture is a privileged site for understanding the changing character of 'intellectual labor' in capitalist development," the above position suggests that architecture is privileged precisely because it complicates but does not eradicate what we take to be intellectual work. It looks like making, it involves making, it yields made things, but it isn't making. It might actually model other "intellectual" disciplines where making is less obvious and latent.

Third, it separates the discourse of emancipation as I have indicated earlier, from that of consumption and links it to one of production. Whether one emphasizes the lessons that Tafuri learned from the Operaist movement regarding the centrality of production over the then (60s) dominant one of accumulation and distribution, or merely reads Tafuri for his consistent emphasis on production, we should not forget these words:

Since an individual work is no longer at stake, but rather an entire cycle of production, critical analysis has to operate on the material plane that determines that cycle of production. In other words, to shift the focus from what architecture wishes to be, or wishes to say, toward what building production represents in the economic game means that we must establish parameters of reading capable of penetrating to the heart of the role played by architecture within the capitalist system. One could object that such an economic reading of building production is other than the reading of architecture as a system of communication. But we can only reply that it will never be repeated too often that, when wishing to discover the secret of a magician's tricks, it is far better to observe him from backstage than to continue to stare at him from a seat in the orchestra.[13]

Contemporary architecture's typical attention to consumption instead of production can and should be seen in the context of capitalism's own historical development, from nineteenth century concentration on production to twentieth century focus on consumption and service.[14] Indeed, one could say that this is neo-liberalism's particular ideological success: it deflects our attention away from labor and does so (learning from Althusser) via autonomy (let's talk about how great architecture looks!). Whatever one might think about theories that foreground labor over consumption—old or crude Marxism?[15]—one cannot deny that this vital aspect of architecture, or its ability to serve an emancipatory good, has been overlooked. Immaterial work is a key to reformulating our identity away from greedy chasers of any job capitalists will throw our way toward a thoughtful stewardship of a sustainable, fair and democratic built environment. It does not preclude design; it suggests that design is a form of thought.

There is a relationship between this thought and my original plea for persuasion, to which I will now return as a form of conclusion. How do we theorist/intellectuals call architects to emancipatory work? If ideology "interpellates"/calls the subject, we then must call her back. If aesthetics and autonomy is the seductive form that ideology's call takes, we must redefine aesthetics to lure the subject past its surface attraction to the deeper agenda embedded in its production, distribution and consumption. (Here I agree with Libero.)

We intellectuals-cum-theorists call to intellectuals-cum-practitioners from a position of equality and solidarity. The equality resides in the lack of distinction between knowledge and design work and in the common identification as workers. The solidarity comes from the class identification that may not yet be apparent to those in the discipline but is waiting to be revealed. If relative autonomy gives us one thing, it is the recognition that our subsystem functions like no other; all of us engaged in it have a common stake and shared access to its protocols. There is nothing to be gained by us pointing fingers at intellectuals or designers who don't "get it", what ever "get it" implies. It makes those of us who criticize other "Leftist" critical thinkers for not being radical enough look cranky, petty and above those we talk to. It is not that those certain architects/intellectuals who don't get it are wrong; they just haven't been given the opportunity to feel secure in what is right. This is my aggravation with Erik's all or nothing position, even as I feel indebted to his insights.

At the same time, I feel that all of us here are struggling to find a position that acknowledges Tafuri's incredibly sharp analysis of architecture's doomed condition in capitalism while not succumbing wholly to its seeming fatalism—that as long as we are in a capitalist system, there is no emancipatory hope for architecture. We all locate the potential for not succumbing in different places, but I think these are disagreements about tactics of persuasion, not of right and wrong. We are all fighting the good fight.

8

But What About Left Architecture?

Erik Swyngedouw

We should re-invent utopia. But in what sense? There are two false meanings of utopia. One is this old notion of imagining an idea of society, which we know will never be realized. The other is the capitalist utopia in the sense of new and new perverse desires that you are not only allowed but even solicited to realize. The true utopia is when the situation is so without issue, without a way to resolve it within the coordinates of the possible that out of the pure urge of survival you have to invent a new space. Utopia is not kind of a free imagination; utopia is a matter of innermost urgency. You are forced to imagine it as the only way out, and this is what [is needed] today.[1]

Politics of Architecture or the Architectural Political?

This morning, twelve journalists of Charlie Hebdo were cold-bloodedly murdered in the Parisian offices of the satirical magazine by two Jihadi's that surely hoped to come closer to God's love with a few souls of infidels under their belt. This was followed quickly by the tasteless recuperation of the attack in most of the elite liberal and self-styled cosmopolitan media, further re-enforcing an antagonistic identitarian friend-enemy configuration. It made starting writing this contribution so much harder. How to think, let alone practice, the possibility for an emancipatory Left architecture when the very fabric that nurtures—even under often difficult circumstances—critical, progressive, and left thought and practice to flourish is so brutally attacked, when the specter of an egalitarian and inclusive utopia recedes even further. Not that I am in Paris myself. In fact, I am looking out of the window of my temporary Thessaloniki flat at the remains of the ancient Roman Forum, an architectural and urbanistic masterpiece that still reminds us today of the foundational spatialities of democratic encounter, while all around it the perverse socio-spatial destruction of the urban fabric under the Troika's austerity urbanism rips the guts out of the city and its people. Many of my Greek architecture and planning colleagues in the mean time are inscribing themselves in a re-invigorated critical left practice, symbolized by the extra-ordinary success of the radical left SYRIZA party in the elections of January 2015.

The above vignettes frame much of the argument that will follow. The aporia that encircles the deadlock of our present situation resides, I believe, precisely in the architectonics of violence that pits identitarian allegiances against neo-liberal cosmopolitan inclusion in the production of a world ruled by the specter of the money sign. Despite their apparent opposition, they are, as Slavoj Žižek keeps reminding us, two sides of the same fake coin, engendering each other in an abyssal violent spiral that requires urgent and radical transgression.[2]

This deadlock is also mimicked by the irreducible void perceptible in the gap between the penetrating but impotent powers of present-day presumably radical architectural and urban theorizations on the one hand (such as this one and others in this book) and the poverty of progressive architectural or urbanistic interventions on the other. This became strikingly clear on 6 December 2014, when a round table discussion was held at the Architectural Association in London on the theme 'How is Architecture Political?'[3] Pier Vittorio Aureli, among others, engaged this question that articulated around the work of political theorist Chantal Mouffe on 'the political' and her defense of an agonistic politics as the premise for a democra-tizing political sequence. Not surprisingly, the participants in the round table also debated at great length many of the themes that this book and its authors address. In his contribution, Aureli reminded us of how any political project is of necessity a spatial one, and any spatial project is of necessity a political one. This is precisely what I insisted on in my earlier contribution of the insurgent architects that animated recent urban rebellions performatively staged: the socio-spatial practices of the occupied and transformed squares and other public spaces constituted a potential political event, understood as the interruption of the givens of the situation and the presentation cum tentative demonstration of a new sense, a new egalitarian way of ordering bodies and functions in time and across space. In doing so, these spatial practices registered how the 'police', understood in the Rancièrian sense, as the condition and process through which places and functions are spatially distributed within an established order, a situational given, on the one hand, and 'the political' as the interruption of that order by rendering audible, perceptible, and visible those who do not count under the paradoxical presupposition of the empty universal of equality on the other.[4] It is precisely this irreducible gap between 'politics' and 'the political' that requires foregrounding in considering the relationship between architecture and politics, between a politics of architecture and the architectural political. As Henri Lefebvre already noted a long time ago, space plays a central and paradoxical role in choreographing the interplay between depoliticization and the 'moment of politics.'[5] Not registering this chasm and its implications reproduces the political deadlock we are in rather than transgressing its stifling repetition.

In his presentation, Aureli explored the paradoxical thesis that 'architecture cannot be political' and that 'architecture is always political', yet the 'politics of the gap' between these two utterances remains suspended, ignoring the radical theoretical and practical disjuncture between architecture's politics and the architectural political. Of course, architectural practices (and architects) are always inserted within the circuits of the police, the theatres of public decision-making, the registers of what is acceptable and not-acceptable, the circulations of capital, materials, and bodies, the relations and practices of power that suspend the egalitarian presupposition of equality, even and precisely at its most performative when architects yet again announce 'the shock of the new'. In this sense, architecture is an integral part of what Jacques Rancière calls the Police. Yet, at the same time, critical architectural and urban thought is replete with analyses of the intransient power of capital, the exclusionary performances of state bureaucracies, and the multiple power choreographies that infuse the capillary power relations of everyday life. In doing so, our theories articulate and account for class and other power dynamics that prevent—often by all means possible—the becoming world of a different socio-spatial ordering. From this rather theoretical perspective, architecture (at least in some of its theoretical architectonics) can also lay claim to be 'political'. Nonetheless, these critical perspectives, I maintain, have now become an integral, if not vital legitimizing, conduit that sustains the deadlock. This is particularly acute when architects claim to translate, without proper politicizing mediation, theoretical analysis to architectural practice.[6]

In what follows, I shall explore some of the issues the other contributors engaged with, namely the question of politicization that Aureli's architecture of autonomy poses and that Libero Andreotti so carefully dissects, the contours for a politicizing Left architecture today, one that can only operate under the name of re-invented communism after the death of socialism, a theme also raised by David Cunningham. And, finally, while architecture may be in a political deadlock, the proliferation of insurgent architects points at a possible horizon for a new radical urbanity.

Consider, for example, how in his *The Project of Autonomy: Politics and Architecture Within and Against Capitalism,*[6] Aureli's excavation of Italian Operaismo (Workerism) as forms of militant intervention subtracted from the state through which communism as an immanent potential unfolding appears within the working class-led dynamics of capitalism itself. The latter operates in particular through the socialization of the collective intellect as a new and key productive force that would render the oppressive power of capital obsolete and put in its place the autonomous and self-managed collective labor of the socialized intellect. The unbearable lightness of being communist, refracted by Aureli into a project for an architecture of autonomy, is one that nonetheless remains fully within the contours of the existing situation, while draped in a radical rhetoric. His invocation of Vienna's radical post WW I socialist worker's housing projects as an example of an architecture of autonomy is a case in point. It is plainly surprising how his analysis ignores how it was precisely Red Vienna's wider radical political configuration, underpinned by a broadly socialist and communist set of practices in a wide range of life world domains, that permitted the deployment of a radical architecture. These interventions violently ruptured the established elite urban fabric and challenged a conservative national state government, a conflict that would in 1938 erupt in physically violent clashes whereby the architectural condition of the great people's housing projects served as militarized defense spaces. The bullet holes in the walls of some of the buildings still testify today, silently, to the political clashes these insurgent architects and their progressive allies had prefigured in the architectonic and social forms of the projects. Equally surprising is Aureli's discussion of Aldo Rossi's view "that there was a possibility of looking at the city as an arena of decisive and singular events whose defined forms could pose a challenge to the urban phenomena and flux surrounding them"[7] as an evocation of the *operaist* legacy in Rossi's work, ignoring the vitally important universalizing politicization that underpins every emancipatory political sequence. The singular event of agonistic interruption, the passage *à l'acte*, remains an hysterical, and thus impotent, act in the absence of a politicizing sequence that articulates around the possibilities for an ega-libertarian, communist, horizon. It is precisely the hard, slow, and difficult process of assembling heterogeneous actors (including architects and urbanists) around a political and radical emancipatory sequence that maintains fidelity to the inaugural event. It is precisely such sequence that retroactively inscribes the event as a 'political' one. For example, the agonistic urban interventions exemplified by the tent-camps of insurgent architects, the designers and builders of 'slum' houses, the re-ordering of space and time in spaces where undocumented immigrants in the West's cities carve out a precarious life while insisting on their utterances to be recognized as a legitimate political voice, could be conceived of as 'evental' sites. Yet, their potential to a politicizing performativity resides in the process of universalization, of producing a new socio-spatial common sense, of mobilizing, assembling, symbolizing, and militantly organizing an emancipatory political sequence. It is to the modalities of such political sequence that I now turn.

As in my first contribution, I maintain that registering what Paul Ricœur first called 'the political paradox'[8] between the in-egalitarian instituted order and the recurrent modalities of its interruption needs to be foregrounded and the violence that political practices of necessity inflict on the process of re-ordering space recognized fully. Indeed, one of the centrally disavowed conditions of contemporary post-political urbanity is the violence inscribed in its practices, and a reminder of course that any urbanistic or architectural intervention is of necessity a violent one, symbolically, materially, and socially. And indeed, on occasion physically as the architectonics of modern drone-warfare and related urbicide keep reminding us.[9] The architects of the Vienna Social Housing projects, for example, readily acknowledged that the violent re-arrangement of space inflicted by a confident national bourgeoisie, that soon would join forces with Nazi Germany, could only be countered by being fully cognizant of the need for formidable and militant opposition, one embedded in the architectonics of the socialist housing projects themselves.

Enacting the communist polis

The Real of the political cannot be fully suppressed and, I claim, returns presently, and among many other experimental politicizing practices, in the form of the urban insurgencies with which I opened my first contribution. If the political is foreclosed and the polis as political community moribund in the face of the post-politicizing suspension of the democratic, what is to be done? What design for the reclamation of the polis as an emancipatory political space can be thought? How and in what ways can the courage of the urban collective intellect(ual) be mobilised to think through a design of and for dissensual or polemical spaces. I would situate the tentative answers to these questions in three interrelated registers of thought.

The first revolves around transgressing the fantasy that sustains the post-political order. This would include, as Žižek maintains, not surrendering to the temptation to act. The hysterical act of resistance ('I have to do something or the city, the world, will go to the dogs') just answers the call of power to do what you want, to live your dream, to be a 'responsible' citizen. Acting is actually what is invited, an injunction to obey, to be able to answer to 'What have you done today?'. The proper response to the injunction to undertake action, to design the new, to be different (but which is already fully accounted for within the state of the situation), is to follow Bartleby's modest, yet radically transgressive, reply to his Master, 'I'd prefer not to ...'.[10] The refusal to act, to ask what they want from me, to want to be liked, to answer the call of power, is not only an affirmation that the Master does not exist or, at least, that the emperor is naked, but also an invitation to think, or rather, to think again.

The courage of the urban intellect(ual) is a courage to be an organic intellectual—in the Gramscian sense—of the city *qua polis*. This is an urgent task and requires the formation of new imaginaries and the resurrection of thought that has been censored, scripted out, suspended, and rendered obscene. In other words, is it still possible to *think*, for the twenty-first century, the design of a democratic, polemical, equitable, free common urbanity, a communist polis? What is required is an urban thinking that moves beyond the critique of what is, and does not consider resistance to be the horizon of what is possible. Can we still think through today the censored metaphors of equality, communism, living-in-common, solidarity, ega-libertarian political democracy? Are we condemned to rely on our humanitarian sentiments to manage socially to the best of our techno-managerial abilities the perversities of late-capitalist urbanity, or can a different politics and process of being-in-common be thought and designed?

The second moment of reclaiming the polis revolves around re-centring/redesigning the urban as a democratic political field of dissensus. This is about enunciating dissent and rupture, and the ability to literally open up spaces that permit voicing and articulating claims, and stage a place in the order of things by and for 'the part of no-part'. This centres on rethinking equality politically; i.e. thinking equality not as a sociologically verifiable concept or procedure that permits opening a policy arena that will remedy the observed inequalities (utopian/normative/moral) some time in a utopian future (i.e. the standard recipe of left-liberal urban policy prescriptions), but as the axiomatically presupposed, albeit contingent, condition of and for the democratic. This must include of course the constitution and construction of common spaces as collectivized spaces for experimenting and living differentially, to counter 'the hyper-exploitation or the time that is imposed and that one tries to reappropriate.'[11] Political space emerges thereby as the collective or common space for the institutionalisation of the social (society) and equality as the foundational gesture of political democracy (presumed, axiomatic, yet contingent foundation).

This requires extraordinary designs (both theoretically and materially) that cut through the master signifiers of consensual urban governance (creativity, sustainability, growth, cosmopolitanism, participation, etc.) and their radical metonymic re-imagination.[12] Such metonymic re-registering demands thinking through and practicing the city as a space for accommodating equalitarian difference and disorder. This hinges critically on creating ega-libertarian public spaces. Most importantly, the utopian framing that customarily informs urban visioning requires reversal to a temporal sequence centred on imagining concrete spatio-temporal utopias as immediately necessary and realisable. This echoes of course Henri Lefebvre's clarion call for the 'Right to the city' understood as the 'Right to the production of urbanisation', one that urges us to think of the city as a process of collective co-design and co-production, a process sustained by insurgent architects.[13]

Thirdly, and most importantly, trans-mutating insurgency into a political sequence poses the need to traverse the fantasy of the elites, a fantasy that is sustained and nurtured by the perverse imaginary of an autopoietic world, the hidden-hand of market exchange that self-regulates and self-organises, serving simultaneously the interests of the Ones and the All, the private and the common. The socialism for the elites that structures the contemporary city is Really one that engages the common and the commons in the interests of the elite Ones through the mobilisation and disciplinary registers of post-democratic politics.[14] It is a fantasy that is further sustained by a double fantastic promise: on the one hand, the promise of eventual enjoyment— 'Believe us and our designs will guarantee your enjoyment'. It is an enjoyment that is forever postponed, that becomes a veritable utopia, a no-place. On the other hand, there is the recurrent promise of catastrophe and disintegration if the elite's fantasy is not realised, if one does not surrender to the injunctions of the Master. This dystopian fantasy is predicated upon the relentless cultivation of fear (for ecological disintegration and ecocide, excessive migration, terrorism, economic-financial collapse), fears that are both relayed by and managed through technocratic-expert knowledge and elite governance arrangements. This fantasy of catastrophe has a castrating effect—it sustains the impotence for naming and designing truly alternative cities, truly different emancipatory spatialities and urbanities.

Traversing elite fantasies requires the intellectual and political courage to imagine egalitarian democracies, the production of common values and the radical re-imagination of the collective production of the greatest collective *oeuvre*, the city, the inauguration of new political trajectories of living life in common, and the courage to choose, to take sides. Most importantly, traversing the fantasy of the elites means recognising that the social, economic, and ecological catastrophe that is announced everyday as tomorrow's threat is not a promise, not something to come, but *is* already the Real of the present.

What is left to think?

We are living in times that are haunted and obsessive in equal measure. On the one hand, our time is haunted by the spectre of once 'really existing socialism'. The idea of communism is indeed tainted by the failure of its twentieth century manifestation, a condition that, towards the end of the previous century, left the Left in a state of utter paralysis, politically and intellectually. This is not to say that the 'obscure disaster'[15] of twentieth century communism does not require urgent and critical attention. On the contrary, this is one of the tasks ahead, one that has to be undertaken in light of the communist hypothesis that a different order is not only possible but also necessary. But in equal measure are we living in obsessive times, obsessive commitments to 'do something', 'to act' in the names of humanity, cosmopolitanism, anti-globalisation or alter-globalisation, the environment, sustainability, liveable cities, climate change, social justice, or other empty signifiers that have become the stand-in to cover up for the absence of emancipatory ega-libertarian political fantasies. The failure of such obsessive activism is now clearly visible. Humanitarianism is hailed to legitimise military intervention and imperial war, the environment becomes a new terrain of capitalist accumulation and serves ideologically as a 'new opium for the masses,'[16] cosmopolitanism is cherished as the cultural condition of a globalised capitalism, and anti-globalisation manifestations have become the predictable, albeit spectacular, short-lived Bakthinian carnivals whose geographical staging is carefully choreographed by the state. Communist thought has disappeared, to be replaced by relentless, yet politically powerless, resistance (rather than transformation), social critique and obsessive acting.

The relationship between our critical urban theories and the political as egalitarian-emancipatory process has to be thought again. It is undoubtedly the case that the three key theoretical and political markers of twentieth century communist politics — state, party and proletariat — require radical reworking. I would insist that neither the state nor the party are any longer of use to think the communist hypothesis. This should not be read as an invitation to ditch new forms of institutional and political organization, to let the common intellect assert itself in a spontaneous self-realizing manner. On the contrary, it calls for a new beginning in terms of thinking through what institutional forms are required at what scale and what forms of political organization are adequate to achieve this. The notion of the proletariat as a political subject equally needs radical overhaul in light of a new critique, not of political economy, but of political ecology. In a context of mass dispossession and privatisation of the commons and the socio-ecological disintegration of life worlds, the political fault lines become drawn around this socio-ecological axis, articulating all manner of new political (proletarian) subjectivities. The name of the 'proletarian' stands here of course for the political subject who, through ega-libertarian struggle, aims to take control again of life and its conditions of possibility.

Communism as a hypothesis and political practice is of course much older than the twentieth century and will, in one guise or the other, re-emerge. Excavating the historical-geographical variations and imaginations of the communist invariant requires re-examining and re-evaluation. Communism as an idea manifests itself concretely each time people come together in-common, not only to demand equality, to demand their place within the edifice of state and society, but also to stage their capacity for self-organization and self-management, and to enact the democratic promise, thereby changing the frame of what is considered possible and revolutionizing the very parameters of state and government, while putting new organizational forms in their place. There are plenty of historical communist political sequences, marking the communist invariant, from the rebellion of the 'ochlos' (the rabble), demanding their rightful place as part of the 'demos' in the governing of the polis in ancient Athens to the French revolutionaries who declared equality and freedom for all in the revolutionary constitution of 1789. Or consider, for example, the 1870 Paris Commune —the first emblematic moment when the proletariat showed, to the horror of the bourgeoisie, their capacity to self-organize and self-govern —, the early Soviets, the Shanghai commune of 1966, brutally smashed by the forces of the Chinese State despite Mao's earlier calls for a permanent revolution (but which had to be performed according to the rules of the State and not taken literally as the Shanghai communards did), or late nineteenth century Canudos, a self-governing mini-state, brutally destroyed by the Brazilian military,[17] and brilliantly immortalised in Vargas Llosa's novel,

8. But What About Left Architecture?

The War of the End of the World.[18]

The key task, therefore, is to stop and think, to think communism again, to think through the communist hypothesis and its actual meaning for a twenty-first century emancipatory, free, and egalitarian politics. The injunction scripted by the communist hypothesis is one that urges communist intellectuals to muster the courage to confront the risk of failing again. There is no alternative. We either manage what exists to the best of our humanitarian abilities or think through the possibilities of re-imagining and realizing the communist hypothesis for the twenty first-century. This will have to take the form of a 'communist geography, a geography of the "real movement which abolishes the present state of things".'[19]

9

The Project of Emancipation, the Communist Hypothesis, and a Plea for *The Platonism of Architecture*

Nadir Lahiji

A specter is haunting Europe — the specter of Communism. All the powers of old Europe have entered into a wholly alliances to exorcise this specter.

—Marx and Engels, *The Communist Manifesto*

When Marx said that the specter of communism was haunting Europe, he meant the hypothesis is here, we have established it.

—Alain Badiou, *The Communist Hypothesis*

We know... that *communism is the right Hypothesis.*

—Alain Badiou, 'Must the Communist Hypothesis be Abandoned?'

Communism is for us not a *state of affairs* which is to be established, an *ideal* to which reality [will] have to adjust itself. We call communism the *real* movement which abolishes the present state of things. The conditions of this movement result from the now existing premise.

—Marx with Engels, *The German Ideology*

Communism is the solution of the riddle of history, and knows itself to be the solution.

—Marx, *Economic and Philosophical Manuscript of 1844*

More than a solution to the problems we are facing today, communism is itself the name of a problem: a name for the difficult task of breaking out of the confines of the market-and-state framework...'
—Slavoj Žižek, *First as Tragedy, Then as Farce*

Preamble

To begin, I pose a maximalist question: Under what parameters might the discourse of architecture intervene in the nexus between "The Communist Hypothesis" and the "Emancipatory Project"? Certain corollary questions follow this one: What do we mean when we say Architecture is an *Idea*? Are the Communist Idea and the Architecture Idea coextensive? Are there any historical conjunctions to be drawn between them? My thesis of *The Platonism of Architecture* is an attempt, albeit incomplete, to answer this question, based on the meaning of 'the Idea' in contemporary radical philosophy. To this idea of Idea I come back later. Here, some preliminary definitions are in order.

First, the "Communist Hypothesis," or the "Communist Idea": a politico-philosophical term developed by Alain Badiou with Slavoj Žižek in the past four years. Badiou claims that humanity, in abstract sense, knows that "*communism is the right hypothesis*. Indeed, there is no other, or at least I am not aware of one. All those who abandon this hypothesis immediately resign themselves to the market economy, to parliamentary democracy—the form of state suited to the most monstrous inequalities."[1]

Second, inseparable from the first, the term "Emancipatory Politics," historically linked to the project of the Enlightenment whose 'political sequences' according to Badiou, go from the French Revolution to May '68, and the long series of *failed* revolutions from China to Iran to the Arab Spring—each one trying, as Samuel Beckett would say, to 'fail better'.

But if, thanks to these and other recent events, the word

137

"communism" is back in circulation, what meaning should we give it?, Badiou asks. He offers one, particularly strong definition in the penultimate chapter of his best bestseller, *The Meaning of Sarkozy*—in the original French, *De quoi Sarkozy est il le nom?*— entitled "Must the Communist Hypothesis Be Abandoned?" He begins by saying "communism is what Kant called an 'Idea,' with a regulatory function, rather than a program."[ii] "Communism" for Badiou is a heuristic hypothesis:

> If it is still true, as [Jean-Paul] Sartre said, that every "anti-communist is a swine," it is because any political sequence that, in its principles or lack of them, stands in formal contra-diction with the communist hypothesis in its generic sense has to be judged as opposed to the emancipation of the whole of humanity, and thus to properly human destiny of humanity. Whoever does not illuminate the coming-to-be-of humanity with the communist hypothesis—whatever words they use, as such words matter little—reduces humanity, as far as its collective becoming is concerned, to animality.[2]

The contemporary capitalist name for this animality is "compe-tition." Badiou asserts that "as a pure Idea of equality" the communist hypothesis has existed since States have existed. However, already by the time of the French revolution, "the communist hypothesis inaugurates political modernity."[3] According to Badiou, since the fall of the *ancien régime*, the communist hypothesis was in no way tied to the "democratic" forms reflected in present-day parliamentarism. "That is indeed why Marx, giving materialist foundations to the first effective great sequence of the modern politics of emancipation, both took over the word 'communism' and distanced himself from any kind of democratic 'politicism' by maintaining, after the lesson of the Paris Commune, that the bourgeois state, no matter how democ-ratic, must be destroyed."[4] In this respect, Badiou points out,

May '68 and the five years that followed it "inaugurated a new sequence for a genuine communist hypothesis, one that always keeps its distance from the State."[5]

The Communist Idea must be separated from the disastrous history of the communist movement. As Bruno Bosteels remarks in *The Actuality of Communism*, an inflation of memory has entangled history; the cost of such an over-emphasis on the past has been to postpone "a genuinely critical history of ourselves from the point of view of the present."[6] Rather, it is a "positive anticipation of the future," according to Bosteels, that brings the idea of communism to the fore today. He quotes Isabelle Garo: Communism, she says, "reappearing at the same time that capitalism becomes once more namable, fusing anti- and post-capitalism into a unique positive name that is not a simple negation of its other, communism remains the name of an emancipated future."[7] The "Actuality of Communism," for Bosteels, is neither old fashion party politics nor pure philosophical speculation or dream. On the first point he quotes Badiou when he notes that "Marxism, the workers" movement, mass demonstration, Leninism, the proletarian party, the Socialist state—all these remarkable inventions of the twentieth century—are no longer of practical use. At the theoretical level, they certainly deserve further study and consideration; but at the level of politics, they have become impracticable."[8] It is useless and "impossible" to return to such notions, Badiou believes. Equally impossible, for Badiou, is Negri's 'intelligence of the multitude,' his renewal of a 'democratized party,' as the Trotskyites and Maoists believed. Rather, we are at the opening of a 'new sequence of the communist hypothesis." "The communist hypothesis as such is generic, it is the basis of any emancipatory orientation..."[9]

For Bosteels, "the actuality of communism" transcends the question of its possibility or impossibility. He notices that Badiou took a step back from the Kantian Idea he previously upheld, suggesting that the status of "communist hypothesis" is 'necessarily undecidable.' In Badiou's words:

> The Idea, which is an operative mediation between the real and the symbolic, always presents the individual with something that is located between event and the fact. That is why the endless debates about the real status of the communist Idea are unresolvable. Is it a question of regulative Idea, in Kant's sense of the term, having no real efficacy but able to set reasonable goals for our understanding? Or is it an agenda that must be carried out over time through a new post-revolutionary State's action on the world? Is it a utopia, perhaps a plainly dangerous, and even criminal, one? Or is it the name of Reason in History? This type of debate can never be concluded, for the simple reason that the subjective operation of the Idea is not simple but complex.[10]

In contrast to such unresolvable questions, Bosteels insists on Marx's reference to the "actuality of communism, as in the *real* or *actual* movement that abolishes the present state of things, here reveal[ing] its wide-ranging Hegelian orientation,"[iii] and makes reference to Fredric Jameson's *The Hegel Variation*:

> The word actuality—an English translation more pointed and useful than its German equivalent *Wirklicheit* or reality as such—is a whole Hegelian program; and we can best approach the Hegelian doctrine of immanence by understanding that for Hegel actuality already includes its own possibilities and potentialities; they are not something separate and distinct from it, lying in some other alternate world or in the future. Qua possibility this promise of the real is already here and not simply "possible."[11]

Bosteels' point is that we should perceive communism not as a "utopian not-yet" but rather as 'something that is always already here, in every moment of refusal of private appropriation and in every act of collective reappropriation.'[12] He quotes Žižek: "The ontological background of this leap from "not-yet" to 'always already' is a kind of 'trading of places' between possibility and actuality: possibility itself, in its very opposition to actuality, possesses an actuality of it own."[13]

Filing A Complaint

None of the critical and radical philosophers who participated in two conferences on the Idea of Communism spoke about the problem of architecture—they did not have to. No doubt their focus was the more urgent tasks of radical theory in the face of the dominant liberal-democratic-capitalist consensus—a discourse which, although albeit obliquely related to "cultural capitalism," is not directly itself artistic or architectural. Yet within the discipline of architecture, critics on the Left might find that they have a *responsibility* to face this question, and consider the extent to which Badiou's 'communist hypothesis' can serve to renew a Leftist critique of architecture.

Regrettably, neither the academy nor the intellectual discourse in architecture today has engaged the dialogue of the Left on the Idea of Communism. Architectural discourse remains firmly rooted within, and coopted by, the dynamic of "cultural capitalism," whose exponents blatantly theorize on the function of architecture in a liberal-democratic-capitalist society. But, while their counterparts in philosophy are routinely called 'scoundrels' by Žižek and others on the Left, no such terms exist within the polite, reverential context of architectural critique. For decades, in the name of freeing architecture from old "tired" modernist discourse, architectural critics have imported the critical philosophy of Gilles Deleuze, and before that of Jacques Derrida. Today, many of those same critics, too numerous to name, are arrogantly announcing the end of *radical critique*, triumphantly dismissing the culture of the radical Left inherited from the 1960s. Yet even as we witness a further retrenchment of political critique in architecture, a new revival of the Communist Idea is occurring, mostly in Europe but also occasionally in the US, where in the last four years alone, publications and conferences on this theme have been legion—to name but a few: Alain Badiou, *The Communist Hypothesis* (2008 [2010]); Costas Douzinas and Slavoj Žižek, eds. *The Idea of Communism* 1(2010); Slavoj Žižek, ed. *The Idea of Communism* 2 (2013); Bruno Bosteels, *The Actuality of Communism* (2011); Jodi Dean, *The Communist Horizon* (2012); Boris Groys, *The Communist Postscript* (2009), and most recently, Alain Badiou's *Philosophy and the Idea of Communism: Alain Badiou in Conversation with Peter Engelmann* (2015). These books offer a wealth of philosophical and political resources on the "communist hypothesis," which have yet to be transposed into a *philosophy of building* as the first step for a more ambitious *theory of equality*—as indissociable elements for any genuine emancipatory project, as essential to it as the equally urgent need for a Left critique of architecture's assimilation into neo-liberal capitalism.

This stream of publications begs the question: if, as Badiou claims, "from Plato onwards, Communism is the only political Idea worthy of a philosopher," *what "architectural hypothesis" might align with the "communist hypothesis"?* An 'optimistic' start to answer this question can be found in the opening remarks by Costas Douzinas and Slavoj Žižek to *The Idea of Communism*— from a conference with the same title held in London at the Birkbeck Institute of the Humanities in March 2009. They write: "The long night of the Left is drawing to a close."[14] The bankruptcy of neo-liberal casino capitalism in 2008 means that "the post Cold War complacency is over. The economic crisis has matured into full-fledged political crisis which is de-legitimizing political systems and distancing people from capitalist ideology."[15] No longer can the pronouncement of the "end of history" in 1989, in aftermath of the collapse of the Berlin War, be sustained: history has returned with a vengeance to renew the radical political ideas and the forms of political practice with which the Left has always been linked. "The idea of communism–they write–has the potential to revitalize theoretical thinking and reverse the de-politicizing tendency of late capitalism."[16]

Subscribing to this view, I would wager that an emancipatory architecture would have to address at least two issues: one is the discourse of *equality* developed in radical political philosophy today. This means facing the problematic Žižek refers to as the question of the 'Excluded and Included', and that Rancière memorably terms the "Part of Those With No Part" (more below). Equally essential, however, is the belief that a *philosophy of building equality* can only be embodied in what I call *anonymous architecture*.

The Platonism of Architecture

What do we mean by "the *Idea* of Architecture"? What would be the relation between the Idea of architecture and its Actuality? While these questions only have meaning in a Platonic context, as questions about *the Platonism of architecture*, it is what Marx said about the *actuality* of communism in *The German Ideology*, where he referred to it as "a movement, *real* or *actual*, which *abolishes the present state of things*," "an *ideal* to which reality [will] have to adjust itself," that is perhaps most decisive. For in archi-tectural terms, it simply means that the actuality of the idea of architecture is nothing if it does not *abolish* both the present "state of affairs" *and* the thought of architecture dominant in capitalist societies. To Jameson's saying: "Qua possibility the promise of the real is already here and not simply 'possible'," I say: the possibility of abolishing the capitalist state of archi-tecture is not only possible but *real* and *present* in the *actuality* of its Idea. Bosteels' reference to a passage by Véronique Bergen in his *The Actuality of Communism,* where he questions the Idea/Actuality distinction, is relevant here. Bosteels remarks:

By the disjunction between the idea or the hypothesis and its realization, does one not have recourse to an operation that is doubly problematic, on the one hand, because of the openly declared presuppositions (establish a difference in nature between a concept and the historical figures of its realization), and, on the other hand, because of the ensuing consequences (return to a Kantian scene based on the split of transcendental and the empirical, the intelligible and sensible, the regulative Idea and the fact, or return to the Deleuzian version of the virtual and the actual.[17]

Bosteels also cites Hegel, who makes the same point with much greater eloquence in his *The Encyclopedia Logic:*

Actuality and thought—more precisely the Idea—are usually opposed to one another in a trivial way, and hence we often hear it said therefore that, although there is certainly nothing to be said against the correctness and truth of a certain thought, still nothing like it is to be found or can actually be put into effect. Those who talk like this, however, only demonstrate that they have not adequately interpreted the nature of either of thought or of actuality. For, on the one hand, in all talk of this kind, thought is assumed to be synonymous with subjective representation, planning, intention, and so on; and on the other hand, actuality is assumed to be synonymous with external, sensible existence.[18]

For Bosteels, the actuality of communism "presupposes the immanence of thought and existence, going so far as to accept the much maligned identity of the rational and real, not as a dogmatic given guaranteed by the objective course of history, but as an ongoing and open-ended task for politics."[19] Hegel again: "As distinct from mere appearance, *actuality* being initially the unity of inward and outward, is so far from confronting reason as something other than it, that it is, on the contrary, what is rational through and through; and what is not rational must, for that very reason, be considered not to be actual."[20]

Now, while being mindful not to fall into what Bosteels has called "Speculative Leftism" and leaving the Kantian regulative Idea behind, it is important to turn to Badiou's Platonism.[21] Let us first recall that in Plato's philosophy the Idea, sometimes called *eidos*, is used inconsistently with the word Form.[22] "It is said that Plato's realm of eternal, unchanging Forms derives from Parmenides and it seems clear that Plato favors an Eleatic non-empirical and deductive approach to determining what's really real."[23] In the platonic dialogues, "the theory of Idea, the Idea of Good, the utopian community and the two-worlds metaphysics are presented as common knowledge."[24] Related to the doctrine of Form, "The domain of Ideas, distinct from the domain of physical things, would include not only piety, justice, courage and moderation, but also numerical Ideas like one, two, three, the geometrical Ideas like point, line, plane, and triangle."[25] All these are put in a set of antinomies: "One, two and three are different from each other. The idea of piety, unity, linearity and triangularity are all different from each other but the same at a still higher ideal level since they are all Ideas. So dialectic is a conceptual or, more broadly, intellectual practice that works towards a comprehensive grasp of the relation between things and their defining Ideas, and among Ideas as constituting a domain distinct from that of things."[26]

These are all standard and rather scanty definitions of the Idea and Form in Platonic philosophy, as they persist in various ways through Descartes, Leibniz, Spinoza, and above all, Hegel. In contemporary radical philosophy, however, there are two powerful and conflicting interpretations of the Idea: one is the anti-Platonism of Deleuze, his so-called "overturning" of Plato, the other is the Platonism of Badiou.

Briefly, Deleuze's anti-Platonism rests on his denying the primacy of original and copy, of model over image, and on his "glorifying the reign of simulacra and reflections," as he writes in his *Difference and Repetition*.[27] A simulacrum is an "image without resemblance," which as Livingston explains, is "built not upon similarity or identity, but disparity and difference."[28] It is not *'founded upon* resemblance' but produces its effects. As Livingston further elaborates, "It is constituted not by the similarity of essence or its static repetition, but by an inherently differential network of relations. In this network, Deleuze writes that "repetition already plays upon repetitions, and difference already plays upon differences. Repetitions repeat themselves, while differentiators difference themselves."[29] Deleuze's system of differential networks, as Livingston remarks, is anti-platonic inasmuch as it rejects the "'entire domain that philosophy after Plato will recognize as its own,' including the order of representation 'defined...by an essential relation to the model or foundation." "[Deleuze's] affirming the rights of simulacra, by contrast, allows us to discern *behind* this order another, more chaotic one: an order of pure differences as producing everything that we recognize as similitude, preceding and constituting all identity and representation as such."[30]

Badiou's Platonism stands in complete contrast to such a view. His definition of Form is grounded in Georg Cantor's mathematical set theory, which posited a "manifold" or "set" as "a totality of definite elements which can be united to a whole through a law. By this—Cantor noted—I believe I have defined something related to the Platonic *eidos* or *idea*."[31] For Cantor, set theory addressed the same problem of the One and Many that vexed Plato, and "which divided Parmenides from Heraclitus and was already avidly pursued by the Pythagoreans."[32] Badiou follows Cantor in his reflections on Platonic Form and

Formalization. He writes:

> I believe that if all creative thought is in reality the invention
> of a new mode of formalization, then that thought is the
> invention of a form. Thus if every creative thought is the
> invention of a new form, then it will also bring new possibil-
> ities of asking, in the end, "what is a form?"...Like Plato, who
> first thought this, thinking is the thinking of forms, something
> that he called ideas but they are also the forms. It is the same
> word, *idea*. It is different from Aristotle's thought where
> thinking is the thinking of substance. His parading is the
> animal. For Plato, it's mathematics. Mathematics holds
> something of the secret of thinking... This is the first point. I
> think I hold a fidelity to this idea, but, at the same time, the
> heart of the most radical experience is politics. Politics itself,
> in a sense, is also a thinking through forms. It is the thought
> of arrangement or thought of contrast or the good life. No. It
> is a thinking of form.[33]

This expanded or unified interpretation of the Platonic Idea is a
recurring theme in all of Baidou's work, from his first *Manifestos
for Philosophy* to *The Second Manifesto of Philosophy*, to his most
recent *Logics of Worlds*. His idea of mathematical formalism has
far-reaching consequences not only for philosophy but for a
radical conception of politics, including, as we have seen, the
Communist Idea. As he famously wrote in *Deleuze: The Clamor
of Being*, "there is no doubting the validity of the proverb: 'tell
me what you think of Plato, and I will tell you who you are'."[34]
For Badiou, Platonism is founded not on the notion of
Difference, as in Deleuze, but on the Same. As Peter Hallward
remarks, Badiou's allegiance to Plato is a "defiantly anti-
contemporary gesture" since "all of the major trends in recent
Western philosophy have been hostile to Plato: Nietzsche and
Heidegger most obviously, but equally Wittgenstein and

Popper, the analytic and pragmatist traditions, the post-structuralism associated with Derrida and Deleuze, the neo-Kantian moralism of the 'nouveau philosophes'—even Soviet historical materialism."[35]

In *The Communist Hypothesis*, Badiou writes: "I call an 'idea' an abstract totalization of the three basic elements: a truth procedure, a belonging to history, and individual subjectivation. A formal definition of the Idea can immediately be given: an Idea is the subjectivation of an interplay between the singularity of a truth procedure and representation of History."[36] Further: "We will say that an Idea is the possibility for an individual to understand that his or her participation in a singular political process (his or her entry into a body-of-truth) is also, in a certain way, a *historical* decision. Thanks to the Idea, the individual, as an element of the new Subject, realizes his or her belonging to the movement of History."[37] Thus "the communist Idea is what constitutes the becoming–political Subject of the individual as also and at the same time his or her projection into History,"[38] which then leads him/her to conclude:

> We will therefore assert the following: 'the Idea exposes a truth in a fictional structure. In the specific of the communist Idea, which is operative when the truth it deals with is an emancipatory political sequence, we will claim that "communism" exposes this sequence (and consequently its militants) in the symbolic order of History. In other words, the communist Idea is the imaginary operation whereby an individual subjectivation projects a fragment of the political real into symbolic narrative of a History.[39]

Badiou's assertions, I believe, can help to argue for the Actuality of the architectural Idea, and for its entering the *here* and *now* of History through disrupting and abolishing the present capitalist "state of affairs" in architecture. *The Platonism of Architecture*, in this sense, amounts to an *Ideology*, in the way Badiou intends this term:

> Basically if you really want to understand the tired-out word "ideology," the simplest thing to do is to stay as close as possible to its derivation: something can be said to be "ideological" when it has to do with an idea.[40]

This Platonism of architecture is also a way to underline the necessary 'anonymity' of emancipatory politics, which as Badiou says, "is essentially the politics of the anonymous masses; it is the voice of those with no names, of those who are held in a state of colossal insignificance by the State."[41] An "anonymous architecture" in this sense is coextensive with what Jacques Rancière calls the "Community of Equals," a term that derives from his analyses of the nineteenth century working class thinkers in his great *The Night of Labour, The Ignorant Schoolmaster* and *Staging the People*, books that Badiou described as outlining the first "political sequence" of the communist hypothesis.[42] It is here that Rancière, defying Louis Althusser, wrote: "It is not Man who makes history, but...concrete individuals, those who produce their means of existence, those who fight in the class struggle."[43] Later in his *Disagreement: Politics and Philosophy*, these anonymous masses become "the part with no part," for whom "politics exists through the fact of a magnitude that escapes ordinary measurement,' and that for this reason represent 'nothing and everything.'[44]

I would like to think that through the Idea, as we understand it in contemporary radical philosophy, and as reflected in the problematic discussed in the present collection, architecture might rediscover its platonic essence as an Emancipatory Project. Thus, I task architectural critics, from phenomenologists to postmodern post-poststructuralists, from deconstructionists to self-declared "avant-gardes" followers of Deleuze, from former 'radicals' to Pragmatists to ponder the same validity of the proverb invoked by Badiou: "Tell me what you think of Plato, and I will tell you who you are."

Afterword

Joan Ockman

What she did with me—I must have been eight, or twelve, who
remembers—was to sit me down in the kitchen and take a
straw broom and start furiously sweeping the floor, and she
asked me which part of the broom was more elemental, more
fundamental, in my opinion, the bristles or the handle. The
bristles or the handle. And I hemmed and hawed, and she
swept more and more violently, and I got nervous, and finally
when I said I suppose the bristles, because you could after a
fashion sweep without the handle, by just holding onto the
bristles, but couldn't sweep with just the handle, she tackled
me, and knocked me out of my chair, and yelled into my ear
something like, "*Aha*, that's because you want to *sweep* with the
broom, isn't it? It's because of what you want the broom *for*,
isn't it?" Et cetera. And that if what we wanted a broom for was
to break windows, then the *handle* was clearly the fundamental
essence of the broom, and she illustrated with the kitchen
window, and a crowd of domestics gathered; but that if we
wanted the broom to sweep with, see for example the broken
glass, sweep sweep, the bristles were the thing's essence. No?
—David Foster Wallace, *The Broom of the System*

Nadir invited me to be the broom of this discussion and I am
honored and flattered and also not a little uncomfortable to be in
the position of having the last word. Plus I'm having a hard time
deciding whether to use the bristles to sweep the floor or the
handle to break windows.

I am going to come down on the side of the bristles, but first
want to vent. Part of the problem as I see it is the nature of the
discourse, the fact that we academics are talking to ourselves,

however heady and engaging this round-robin. Just as useful as another statement of position at this point might be a word cloud. What it would prove to anyone who cares to listen in on our interchange is, first, the circumscribed universe in which we are operating and, second, how frustrated all of us are by the impasse in which we find ourselves within the present culture of architecture. So we are earnestly sifting through available theories, mobilizing our respective rhetorics, searching for means to talk/write our way into or out of the problem — in short, to find a way not to answer "no" to the Question that Nadir has posed.

With this bit of impoliteness out of my system, so to speak, I hasten to add that there could be worse uses of our collective time. The four interlocutors with whom I am asked to parley here have much, much of importance and interest to say. Because I am still, inexcusably, underread in some of the more recent bibliography that occupies space in our shared word cloud (I confess that Nadir had to explain to me exactly what "radical philosophy" connotes today), I will of necessity confine myself to clarifying questions, reacting to some arguments my colleagues have presented, and finally offering some thoughts on a subject to which I've given some serious reflection over the years, namely the devastating analysis of Manfredo Tafuri, and especially how to move beyond it.

Let me first back up to the initial Question:

Can architecture be an emancipatory project?

to which it is immediately necessary to append the qualifier:

Can architecture be an emancipatory project under capitalism?

and further (leaving implicit for the moment what is meant by emancipation):

Can architecture be an emancipatory project if it remains an object of consumer and celebrity culture?

Can architecture be an emancipatory project if it is complicit with financial speculation and the real estate industry?

Can architecture be an emancipatory project if it is the handmaiden of hegemonic power?

Can architecture be an emancipatory project if it continues to have an oblivious or predatory relationship to increasingly fragile environmental and material resources?

Since all of the above "if" clauses are, in fact, not hypotheticals but *faits accomplis*, it seems more useful for our purpose to reformulate the Question as:

How can architecture be an emancipatory project if it... ?

Such a reformulation has the advantage of shifting the Question from the putative to the practical realm, from philosophy to strategy. "The philosophers have only interpreted the world in various ways; the point is to change it."[1] But hold on, I'm getting ahead of myself.

I

I would like to take David's two extremely cogent and well-nuanced contributions as a point of departure. I find myself in almost total agreement with everything he writes, except for his conclusion, which consists of a rather vague claim that architecture, simply by playing "its own messy, complex, contradictory role" (shades of Robert Venturi?), will partake in a "contemporary *metropolitan* politics of emancipation and transformation" (his italics).

I will focus on David's second contribution, underscoring a few things that especially resonate for me. First, that the autonomy of the political is a theoretical fallacy and an actual impossibility since, as he succinctly puts it, "capital over-determines modern social relations, *including politics*." As David makes clear, the notion of bracketing off the political sphere from the economic one in order to operate out of a hermetic critical enclave is wishful thinking. While the impulse to construct such an enclave represents an authentic utopian desire and is also an inspiring thought-experiment—as Fredric Jameson, in the wake of Ernst Bloch, would insist—there is at present no capitalism-free vantage point from which to occupy a place of Great Refusal. (If Aldo Rossi truly exemplified such a position, how did Alessi sell so many coffeepots?) Moreover, it is precisely the *interrelationship* between the political and the economic that is at stake. Despite its originality, the recent autonomy-of-the-political discourse in architecture, put forward most boldly by Pier Vittorio Aureli (and endorsed, with qualifications, by Libero), not only has nostalgic roots in a particular Italian Communist Party politics of the 1970s that is of questionable relevance today, as David notes, but—and here is where Libero takes his distance—it becomes a mirror image of the logic of the contemporary capitalism it attacks. In its recourse to the sublime and unrepresentable (latter-day Hilberseimer, Superstudio), the polemical architecture of the anti-spectacle "does not so much critically reconfigure" the spectacle, Libero writes perceptively, as offer a new image of "seduction and fear, attraction and repulsion."

Furthermore, and this probably does not get emphasized by anyone sufficiently, the revalorization of the political "*tout court*"—a revealing locution, on its way to becoming a tic—gives primacy to a sphere in which ideology reigns almost by definition (the political always has a politics...), which carries its own contradictions and problems, as the shotgun marriage of "Karl and Carl" (Marx and Schmitt) makes all too plain.

A second critique leveled by both David and Libero with which I concur concerns Erik's faith in disruptive, or "insurgent," architectural practices. As I began by indicating, I fully share Erik's impatience with architectural theory, an intellectual field rendered impotent by academicization more than a generation ago. Ironically, after having *no* theory for a very long time (at least in the U.S.), the discipline of architecture not only prostrated itself to theory's over-sophistications in the 1970s and '80s, but, in the era of Reagan/Thatcher neo-conservatism, lent itself, in the names of postmodernism and post-structuralism, to a depoliticizing agenda. Ever since, theory in architecture has tended to serve as an alibi or intellectual surrogate for serious and sustained social-political thought.

I must agree with David, though, that beyond Erik's lack of much specificity as to what sorts of performative "socio-spatial" practices he has in mind, such happenings cannot be detached from the larger infrastructures out of which they emerge, especially when it comes to the built environment, where "material instantiations of a certain socio-economic 'practico-inert' become of paramount importance," as David wordily puts it. Nor can these explosive and unscripted events be prevented from being absorbed by the global system into which they erupt, especially in our present media society.

Once again, such emblematic events enact, at times in the most dramatic possible way, real desires. Yet after the festival comes Monday morning, and the fool who was crowned philosopher-king becomes fool again. The subsiding of the Occupy movement, like the unintended consequences that followed the Arab Spring, offers a cautionary tale for revolutionary ardor—the present generation's equivalent of '68?—and at the very least suggests much slower and more unpredictable scenarios of transformation. The "alarm clock that in each minute rings for sixty seconds" eventually winds down or ceases to be heard.[2] Erik acknowledges the necessity of "trans-mutating insurgency into a political sequence." What kind of sequence exactly? Who are the courageous actors—who also have to eke out a living as architects (we're still talking about architects here, I presume) and feed their families in today's increasingly precarious circumstances—likely to be? Without a strategy for prolonging the salutary shock of defamiliarization beyond first blush, without a plan not just for mobilizing oppositional impulses but for sustaining them in other forms—in short, without a process of institutionalization that is well- plotted and (above all) democratic—the effects of the kind of actions to which Erik exhorts us are likely to be short-lived or to get hijacked.

II

The "right to the city" that Erik seeks to assert through militant singularities has a perfect inversion in the counterrevolutionary practices of the contemporary "creative class." While the demands of the latter are more likely to take the form of an expectation that there be a Starbucks and a gym on each street corner, the maverick mobilities and hip informalities of this "class" are characteristic of the new spirit of capitalism, as described by Boltanski and Chiapello in their eponymous book.[3] Such activities revolve around forms of employment that are increasingly project-based—a type of labor that has been familiar to architects for a very long time, given the feast-or-famine realities of architectural commissions—and ride on the new electronic connectivities that make a "networked" labor force of this type efficient and productive. Perversely, as plenty of commentators have pointed out, the restructured work environment is justified by capitalist management as a new type of freedom, despite the insecurities built into the new arrangements, which have a particularly brutal impact on younger workers.

From this perspective, Peggy constructively redirects us back to architecture in its normative professional setting and disciplinary understanding, as well as to the figure of the architect her/himself. Peggy's Question might be reframed as:

How can architects have an emancipatory project?

She also calls our attention, in Benjaminian fashion, to the issue of the architect as a producer, and to the relations between production and consumption. Forgoing the romanticism of the architectural "project," another way of putting her Question might be:

Can architecture be an emancipatory product?

The answer depends on whether we continue to understand the products of architecture as objects ready for consumption, originating at the moment when the camera photographs the living room with the vase of flowers on the coffee table—in other words, when the commodity fetish starts asserting itself in all its topsy-turvy illogic—or whether we understand them as resultants of complex, multi-authorial processes of making. The latter would encompass not just the initial meeting of minds between architect (or team of architects) and client over a design, but also a much larger constellation of material and immaterial circumstances and events, including the extraction of raw materials from their source, their industrial processing, their assembly by a succession of workers on the construction site, the project's financial instrumentation, its representations and documents, and much else.

Writing from the standpoint of both the architectural practitioner and educator, Peggy aptly inquires "how we [i.e., we architects] can presume to offer successful spatial gifts to society when we do not recognize our shared identity (as citizens/workers) with those who would build them or benefit from them." In posing this implicitly "who's we, white man?" question, she also wonders "how we can recognize what constitutes 'emancipatory' if we've never experienced [it] in our own work/lives." What she is suggesting is that to produce emancipated architecture, architects must first clean their own house. Quoting Peggy again:

> How can a flawed institution based on sexism, racism, and hierarchical social status expect even to conceive of let alone produce liberating spaces?

On the other hand, less convincing from the perspective of "emancipation" are Peggy's pleas for professional solidarity, for "sharing and cooperation." While admirably idealistic, such liberal-ethical sentiments have an unmistakable whiff of soft politics about them. More welcome are her practical policy reform proposals, although so long as they remain piecemeal they too do not seem up to the task of counteracting the large and amorphous institutional edifice that is the contemporary culture of architecture. It is here that Libero's strictures concerning the necessity "to understand clearly the workings of power" and "to imagine, and as far as possible to practice, an alternative based on a theory of human nature as best we understand it" are more to the point.

III

It is striking how much the critique first made by Tafuri close to half a century ago continues to stick in our respective craws, mine included. "Architecture as politics is by now such an exhausted myth," as the Venetian historian wrote witheringly in 1980 in the introduction to *The Sphere and the Labyrinth*, "that it is pointless to waste any more words on it."[4] Tafuri's unequivocal verdict on the historical avant-gardes of the 1920s was handed down in the disillusioning aftermath of the activism of the 1960s and amid the hedonistic escapades of the neo-avant-gardes of the '70s. "Upon awakening," Tafuri sternly admonished both utopian dreamers and escape artists in the last sentence of the same book, "the world of fact takes on the responsibility of reestablishing a ruthless wall between the image of estrangement and the reality of its laws."[5]

Is there any greater prospect of transcending the ironclad reality principle today than there was in the 1970s? As I have argued elsewhere, it is essential to understand Tafuri's austere and melancholy pronouncements in their historical context.[6] Libero argues something similar, pointing out that if the problem for Tafuri in the early 1970s was to overcome the left-wing optimism of the '60s with its naive "hopes in design," the current problem is to counteract an opportunistic cynicism that, under the triumphal banner of neo-liberalism, has resulted in "post-political" or "post-critical" abandonment and celebration. Yet instead of once again proclaiming a willed Gramscian optimism in the face of an intractable situation—even if there is still reason to do so—let me attempt to take an altogether different tack in exorcising pessimism.

It might go something like this:

Architecture can become an emancipatory project when, and only when, it becomes a necessity, not a luxury.

By this I do not mean to suggest a return to the grand illusions of modern architecture, nor to the subterfuges of "architecture or revolution." (Bear in mind that Le Corbusier's *Vers une architecture* was addressed not only to *Messieurs les Architectes* but also to paternalistic capitalists and benevolent captains of French industry, for whom decent housing was foremost a matter of enhancing the productivity and compliance of their workers; Herbert Marcuse would later term this arrangement "repressive tolerance," a state of existence against which the residents of Le Corbusier's housing at Pessac eventually rebelled.) What I have in mind, in fact, is not even a matter of architectural agency, at least not per se.

I am rather trying to anticipate and imagine how the practice of architecture will change, will have to change, in response to new realities. These realities are already impending as the world continues down the road of hyper-urbanization and as a cascade of environmental disasters created by the current mode of production take further toll. Such conditions—which it does not take a Futurist or a Buckminster Fuller to predict with a degree of certainty in the not far distant future—will require experts who are able to contribute to increasingly consequential kinds of projects and decision-making. And by virtue of their specialized environmental training, architects are likely to be called upon to play a central role.

In this context, it will become more difficult for architecture to remain a trivial pursuit or for architects to go on producing "negligible objects," as Tafuri once put it. The need for adequate housing, for structures to accommodate social services and public institutions, for reconstruction of damaged or threatened urban fabrics, for the overall organization and planning of both proximity and mobility—in short, for the spatial redistribution of planetary resources—will become so great and so urgent that the almighty profit motive will increasingly have to defer to other priorities. Star architecture? A luxury no one will be able to afford.

Perhaps this is the beginning of an answer to David's question of how to restore to architecture the tasks that capitalist development took away from it. Or to Libero's longing for a new New Deal. What neo-liberalism ushered out by the front door might just return by the back. It will not be a simple matter, though, of exchanging the concept of political economy for the more appealing one of political ecology, as Erik proposes. The regime of global finance and the disparities of wealth and poverty will not organically give way to more "ega-libertarian" arrangements. In situations where money is hoarded by those who still have it and resources are scarce, the threat that cities and life itself will devolve into a Darwinian competition for survival will be all the greater. Yet it will also become more difficult for architects to maintain top-down, aestheticized views of grim bottom-up realities. (I cannot help but think here of Rem Koolhaas flying over Lagos in a helicopter borrowed from the Nigerian president, observing how what appeared on the ground to be pure chaos resolved itself from above into "metabolism and flows" and abstract geometric compositions of "red turning into white turning into black."[7])

Is what I am describing an accelerationist theory of reality? I guess so. But I do not think it's apocalyptic science fiction. Those who could be written off as "doomsters" and "eco-freaks" in the '60s and '70s (and even as recently as Al Gore's bid for the American Presidency) have more credibility today. At the same time, it is worth returning to an essay written by Hans Magnus Enzensberger four decades ago, "A Critique of Political Ecology," in which the author warned that the "eco-industrial complex" had already become a growth industry and that stop-gap liberal reforms were failing to touch the roots of the problem, which lay precisely in capitalism and its self-serving ideology: "The knot of the ecological crisis cannot be cut with a paper-knife. The crisis is inseparable from the conditions of existence systematically determined by the mode of production."[8] Similar arguments have been made much more recently by David Harvey and others.[9] Architects, for their part, have become only too familiar (and complicit) today with palliatives like "green-washing" and other purely technological "solutions."

Will architects as a profession be able to rise to the new historical tasks presented to them? It all depends. As Enzensberger noted in 1974 with respect to environmental issues, "A long process of clarification will be necessary before the ecological movement has reached that minimum degree of political consciousness which it would require finally to understand who its enemy is and whose interests it has to defend."[10]

And here is where the transformation of architectural consciousness not only will be sped up by the actual movement of history but must also be broadened and deepened by education. The role of architecture education today must be to prepare future generations of environmental practitioners and urban intellectuals for *le grand jeu à venir*. This is the emancipatory project:

> *Architecture can be an emancipatory project when, and only when, it becomes truly avant-garde.*

I realize this assertion initially sounds preposterous. In the golden age of the creative class, the term *avant-garde* strikes us as either hopelessly commodified—having been appropriated by the branding industry as a synonym for "cutting-edge"—or else a candidate for the dustbin of exhausted twentieth century ideas. Yet in its original military usage the term had little to do with subversiveness and still less with radical chic and claiming one's fifteen minutes of fame—cultural meanings that subsequently accrued to it. Rather, the advance guard of an army had the job of reconnoitering uncharted territory and reporting back to the rest of the troops. It was deputed to scout out what lay ahead. In 1825, in one of the term's earliest semantic transfers, Olinde Rodrigues, a disciple of Saint-Simon and a committed social reformer, stated in a fictive dialogue among an artist, a scientist, and an industrialist, "We, the artists, serve you as avant-garde: the power of the arts is the most immediate and the most rapid." He continued: "What destiny more beautiful for the arts than to exercise a positive influence on society, a true ministry, and to project themselves ahead of all the intellectual faculties in the era of their greatest development!"[11]

There is an evangelizing and also a technocratic subtext to this pronouncement, as to Saint-Simonian socialism itself. As such, I would prefer to replace the word "ministry" with something like "métier." Yet might architecture in the twenty-first century, schooled in both design and science as well as in history, armed with both creative and critical-environmental intelligence, operating at the intersection of material and immaterial labor, and—not least—aware of its social as well as professional responsibilities, fulfill the institutional role once envisaged for an artistic avant-garde? Might a *radically realist* architecture, produced by conscious and conscientious practitioners, yet serve as the broom of a system in need of sweeping change?

As an architectural historian and educator, I have to allow myself to think so.

Notes

Introduction

1. See Maurizzio Lazzarato, *The Making of the Indebted Man* (Los Angeles: Simiotext(e), 2011).
2. Alain Badiou, *The Communist Hypothesis* (London and New York: Verso, 2010), 44.
3. See Siegfried Kracauer, *The Mass Ornament*, trans., ed., and with an introduction by Thomas Y. Levine (Cambridge: Harvard University Press, 1995.
4. See Thomas Y. Levin, 'Introduction,' in ibid.
5. Ibid., 18.
6. Kracauer, 'The Mass Ornament,' ibid., 78.
7. Ibid., 80.
8. Ibid., 84.
9. Levin, ibid., 16.
10. See Slavoj Zizek, *In Defense of Lost Causes* (London and New York: Verso, 2008), 5.

1 Autonomy's Adventures: Or What Does it Mean to Politicize Architecture?

1. See Pier Vittorio Aureli, *The Project of Autonomy: Politics and Architecture within and against Capitalism* (New York, Princeton Architectural Press, 2008).
2. See, for example, Somol and Whiting, "Notes around the Doppler Effect and other Moods of Modernism," in William Saunders, ed., *The New Architectural Pragmatism* (Minneapolis, University of Minnessota Press 2007), 22-33.
3. The recent literature on architectural autonomy is actually quite scarce. See Anthony Vidler, "Autonomy", in *Histories of the Immediate Present: Invention architectural modernism* (Cambridge MASS-London, MIT Press 2008),17-21; Stanford Anderson, "Quasi-Autonomy in Architecture: The Search for

an 'In-between," in *Perspecta* 33 (2002): 30–37, M. Hays, "Introduction" in M. Hays, ed. *Architecture Theory since 1968* (Cambridge MASS-London 2000), x-xi, and Hays, "Abstraction's Appearance (Seagram Building)," in R.E. Somol, ed. *Autonomy and Ideology: Positioning an Avant-Garde in America* (New York, The Monacelli Press 1999), and more recently, David Cunningham, "Architecture and Politics of Aesthetics: Autonomy, Heteronomy and the Philosophy of Art," in Nadir Lahiji, ed., *The Missed Encounter of Radical Philosophy with Architecture* (London: Bloomsbury, 2014). A basic text is Ezio Bonfanti, "Autonomia dell'Architettura" in Luca Sacchetti, ed. *Ezio Bonfanti Scritti di Architettura* (Rome Clup 1981),103-118. This essay, published in the first issue of *Controspazio* (June 1969) and as yet untranslated into English, is the by far the best statement of the *Tendenza*'s position on autonomy from which many of Aureli's arguments derive.

4. Debord, *The Society of the Spectacle* (New York: Zone Books 1994), 143-145. On the chiasmus more generally, see Boris Weiseman and Anthony Paul, eds, *Chiasmus and Culture* (New York and Oxford: Berghahn 2014).

5. Paolo Virno, "Do You Remember Counterrevolution?," in Paolo Virno and Michael Hardt, eds., *Radical Thought in Italy* (Minneapolis and London, University of Minnesota Press 1996).

6. Guy Debord, *Comments on the Society of the Spectacle* (London-New York, Verso 1998) 76.

7. See Owen Hatherley, *Militant Modernism* (Winchester UK and Washington, Zero Books 2008).

8. Vidler, "Autonomy," 20, and Aureli, *The Project of Autonomy*, 60.

9. Quoted in Miles Glendinning, *Architecture's Evil Empire? The triumph and tragedy of global modernism* (London, Reaktion Books 2010), 168.

10. Gar Alperovitz, *America Beyond Capitalism: Reclaiming our Wealth, Our Liberty, and Our Democracy* (New Jersey: Wiley and Sons 2005). Aureli does not elaborate on the political commitments of the *Tendenza*, but see Ezio Bonfanti, "Architettura per I Centri Storici," in Aldo Rossi, et. al. *Architettura Razionale* (Milan Franco Ageli Editore 1975), 189-226.

11. See M. Hays, ed., "Introduction," x: "First and foremost, architectural theory is a practice of mediation. In its strongest form, mediation is the production of relationships between formal analysis of a work of architecture and its social ground or context (however nonsynchronous these sometimes may be), but in such a way as to as to show the work of architecture as having some *autonomous force* with which it could also be seen as negating, distorting, repressing, compensating for, and even producing, as well as reproducing, that context." This methodological definition of autonomy echoes an obsessive theme in Left critical theory: the critique of vulgar Marxism, which was often argued on objective and empirical grounds. Hays cites Jameson on mediation as transcoding, but fails to note the latter's distinction between mechanical and expressive causality— which allows the first kind of direct, coercive causality to apply in particular historical conditions, similar, arguably, from those that hold today. See also Hays, "Hannes Meyer and the Radicalization of Perception" in M. Hays, *Modernism and the Posthumanist Subject* (Cambridge MASS-London, MIT Press 1995), 23-148, and M. Hays, "Abstraction's Appearance," ibid.

12. Adorno, *Aesthetic Theory* (London Routledge and Kagan Paul 1984),154.

13. Pier Vittorio Aureli, *Rome: The Center(s) Elsewhere* (New York Skira 2010).

14. Edward Burtinski, *Manufactured Landscapes* (New Haven Yale

University Press 2003).

15. Massimo Cacciari, *Pensiero negativo e razionalizzazione* (Padova: Marsilio 1977).

16. See Raffaele Liucci's excellent *Il Politico della Domenica: Ascesa e Declino di Massimo Cacciari* (Viterbo: Stampa Alternativa Nuovi Equilibri 2013), a fine example of muckraking architectural journalism. Liucci shows how during Cacciari's tenure as mayor, the one-time Marxist architect turned philosopher oversaw the complete commodification of a city that now draws an unbelievable 22 million people a year, generating vast profits for investors who have poured some of them into rampant speculation on the Lido and on a ten-square mile area called the "Quadrante Tessera" bordering the city center, soon to be dominated by Frank Ghery's sprawling "Venice Gateway," at the same time that more than half the residents of Venice have moved out, nontourist related activities have disappeared, and the environmental damage caused by the huge ferry boat industry has reached a point that UNESCO has threatened to remove Venice from its list of protected World Heritage sites. Cacciari's shady dealings with convicted fraudsters like Don Luigi Verze', his involvement in the nativist politics of the North-eastern region, his rising career as a television personality, not to mention his most spectacular architectural failure, Santiago Calatrava's ungainly and dangerous "fourth bridge" over the Canal Grande, have never occasioned a single expression of regret.

17. Reinhold Martin, *Utopia's Ghost: Architecture and Postmodernism, Again* (Minneapolis-London University of Minnessota Press 2010), xx.

18. Benjamin, "Pariser Brief <I>" in *Gasammelte Schriften*, vol. 3, ed., Hella Tiedemann Bartels (Frankfurt: Suhrkamp, 1972), 482-95.

19. See Andrew Hewitt, *Fascist Modernism: Aesthetics, Politics,*

and the Avant-Garde (Stanford, Stanford University Press 1993), 76.

20. This interpretation goes against a very strong tendency to see the aestheticisation of politics as somehow the result of processes internal to art itself. Peter Burger, Philippe Lacou-Labarthe, and Boris Gorys all subscribe to this basically ahistorical reading. See Lutz Koepnick, *Walter Benjamin and the Aesthetics of Power* (Lincoln and London, University of Nebraska Press 1999),14-24.

21. J. Rancière, *The Politics of Aesthetics* (London, Continuum 2004).

22. On universalism as a weapon for the Left, see "How does the Subaltern Speak? An Interview with Vivek Chibber," in *Jacobin* 10 (Spring 2013).

23. See David Harvey, "The Neo-liberal city" https://www.youtube.com/watch?v=rfd5kHb-Hc8

24. K. Marx, Letters from the *Deutsch-Französische Jahrbücher,* Cologne, May 1843.

2 Architecture, the Built and the Idea of Socialism

1. Manfredo Tafuri, "Preface to the Second Italian Edition", *Theories and History of Architecture,* trans. Giorgio Verrecchia (London: Granada, 1980), unpaginated.

2. Reinhart Kosselleck, *The Practice of Conceptual History: Timing History, Spacing Concepts* (Stanford: Stanford University Press, 2002), pp. 248-264.

3. Manfredo Tafuri, cited in Marco Biraghi, *Project of Crisis: Manfredo Tafuri and Contemporary Architecture,* trans. Alta Price (Cambridge, MA: MIT Press, 2013), p. 27.

4. Alejandro Zaera-Polo et al, *Façade* (Venice: Marsilio, 2014), pp. 3, 200.

5. Tahl Kaminer, Miguel Robles-Duran and Heidi Sohn, Introduction to *Assymetries: Studies and Projects on Neoliberal Urbanization* (Rotterdam: 010 Publishers, 2011), p. 16.

6. See Hal Foster, "The Master Builder", in *Design and Crime (and Other Diatribes)* (London and New York: Verso, 2002).

7. Zaera-Polo et al, *Façade*, pp. 3, 55.

8. One result is that, from this perspective, "architectural emancipation" would entail an emancipation from "architecture" itself.

9. Siegfried Giedeon, *Building in France, Building in Iron, Building in Ferro-Concrete*, trans. J. Duncan Berry (Santa Monica: Getty Centre for the History of Arts and the Humanities, 1995), p. 145.

10. Adam Hollinghurst, "Sculptures in Air", *The Guardian*, August 21st 2004.

11. Jonathan Hill, *The Illegal Architect* (London: Black Dog, 1998), p. 18.

12. On this, see the forthcoming book by Douglas Spencer, *The Architecture of Neoliberalism* (London: Bloomsbury, 2016).

13. Tafuri, *Theories and History of Architecture*, unpaginated.

14. Lukasz Stanek, Introduction to Henri Lefebvre, *Towards An Architecture of Enjoyment*, trans. Robert Bononno (Minneapolis: University of Minnesota Press, 2014), p. xxxv.

15. As Justin McGuirk nicely sums this up in his recent book on Latin American architecture: "This is a familiar story. ... Though rarely the fault of architecture itself—and more often a case of poor maintenance, mismanagement and blighting by poverty—the architects were blamed. Their sins were catalogued and generalized: treating people like ants, making cities ugly, replacing variety with standardization ... Citing 'failure', governments used these sins as an excuse to stop building social housing, relying on the private sector to fill the gap and allowing their neoliberal policies to make cities more unequal places". Justin McGuirk, *Radical Cities: Across Latin America in Search of a New Architecture* (London and New York: Verso, 2014), p. 7.

16. Theodor Adorno, "Functionalism Today", in Neil Leach

(ed.), *Rethinking Architecture: A Reader in Cultural Theory* (London and New York: Routledge, 1997), p. 16.

17. Manfredo Tafuri, *Architecture and Utopia: Design and Capitalist Development*, trans. Barbara Luigia La Penta (Cambridge, MA: MIT Press, 1976), p. 181. This does not mean, of course, that architects can't and shouldn't do better as regards their own working practices, treatment of labor, promotion of gender or racial equality, and so on.

18. Adorno, "Functionalism Today", p. 17.

19. See David Cunningham, "Architecture and the Politics of Aesthetics: Autonomy, Heteronomy and the Philosophy of Art", in Nadir Lahiji (ed.), *The Missed Encounter of Radical Philosophy with Architecture* (London: Bloomsbury, 2014).

20. Patrick Keiller, *The View from the Train* (London and New York: Verso, 2013), p. 70.

21. Manfredo Tafuri, *The Sphere and the Labyrinth: Avant-Gardes and Architecture from Piranesi to the 1970s*, trans. Pellegrino d"Acierno and Robert Connolly (Cambridge, MA: MIT Press, 1987), p. 135.

22. Zaha Hadid, cited at: http://www.theguardian.com/world/2014/feb/25/zaha-hadid-qatar-world-cup-migrant-worker-deaths

23. See David Cunningham, "Metropolitics, or, Architecture and the Contemporary Left", in Nadir Lahiji, ed. *Architecture Against the Post-Political* (London and New York: Routledge, 2014), pp. 11-30.

24. See Pier Vittorio Aureli, *The Project of Autonomy: Politics and Architecture within and against Capitalism* (New York: Princeton Architectural Press, 2008), pp. 50-52.

25. Domenico Losurdo, "The Adventures of the Revolutionary Subject from the 19th to the 21st Century", *Revolution and Subjectivity*, Brumaria 22, Madrid, 2010, p. 96. This is not to concur with the orthodox Leninist "lessons" that Losurdo tends to draw from this.

26. See Alain Badiou, *The Rebirth of History: Times of Riots and Uprisings*, trans. Gregory Elliott (London: Verso, 2012), p.13, citing Marx.

27. Antonio Negri, *Goodbye Mr Socialism: Radical Politics in the 21st Century*, trans. Peter Thomas (London: Serpent"s Tail, 2008), p. 200,

28. As Jameson similarly notes, perhaps, too, "'bureaucracy' itself needs to be rescued from its stereotypes, and reinvoked in terms of the service and class commitment it has had at certain heroic moments of bourgeois society (while reminding people that the largest bureaucracies are in any case those of big business)". Fredric Jameson, *Valences of the Dialectic* (London and New York: Verso, 2007), p. 382.

29. And lest this be thought of as a specific dig at the influence of either currently fashionable post-Althusserian French philosophy or Italian post-autonomia, it should be said that matters are not always much better where attempts to apply either Lefebvre or the Situationists to the present conjuncture are concerned.

30. At its extreme, the resultant "realism" comes to take the form of someone like Patrik Schumacher's writings, which constitute an increasingly explicit affirmation of the free market as itself a self-organizing and self-correcting "process" — both exemplifying a sense that "there is no alternative" to architecture's hitching its cart to capitalist development and a far more general antipathy to the possibility of any process of rational planning that might identify "the most productive mix and arrangement of land uses" (which is instead replaced by the "determinations" of "architecture's private clients"). In Tom Verebes, ed., *Masterplanning the Adaptive City: Computational Urbanism in the Twenty-First Century* (London: Routledge, 2013), p. 120.

31. See Alex Williams and Nick Srnicek, "#Accelerate Manifesto for an Accelerationist Politics", online at:

http://criticallegalthinking.com/2013/05/14/accelerate-manifesto-for-an-accelerationist-politics/;
see also David Cunningham, "A Marxist Heresy? Accelerationism and its Discontents", *Radical Philosophy* 191 (2015): 29-38.

32. Jameson, *Valences of the Dialectic*, pp. 299, 382.

33. McGuirk, *Radical Cities*, p. 16.

34. See Cunningham, "Metropolitics, or, Architecture and the Contemporary Left"; and David Cunningham and Alexandra Warwick, "Unnoticed Apocalypse: The Science Fiction Politics of Urban Crisis", *City* 17, 4 (2013): 433-48.

35. See David Harvey, "Commonwealth: An Exchange", online at:
https://antonionegriinenglish.wordpress.com/2010/09/09/commonwealth-an-exchange-between-david-harvey-and-hardt-and-negri/

36. Immanuel Wallerstein, *Historical Capitalism* (London: Verso, 1983), pp. 109-110.

3 Architects, Really

1. David Harvey, "The Insurgent Architect at Work," in *Readings in the Philosophy of Technology*, David M. Kaplan, ed. (Lanham, Maryland: Rowman and Littelfield Publishers, Inc., 2004).

2. Edward R. Ford, *The Details of Modern Architecture*, vol. 1, (Cambridge MA: MIT Press, 1990), 9.

3. As Paolo Tombesi has pointed out, "the now only vestigial use of fee scales around the world makes the relativity of the entire business even more evident in the face of market pressures: private negotiations in regimes of competition have indeed succeeded in lowering actual work rates below rational thresholds, with plenty of evidence to prove that the payment of architectural labour is detached from the specific measurement of economic time." In his unpublished essay,

"More for Less—Architectural Labour and Design Productivity in the forthcoming, *The Architect as Worker: Immaterial Labor, the Creative Class, and the Politics of Labor,* Peggy Deamer, ed, (London: Bloomsbury, 2015).

4. Tombesi.

5. Erik Olin Wright, *Classes* (London: Verso Books, 1985), 247.

6. For the most part, traditional Marxism had ignored the issue of "creativity" management, having associated creativity only with exploited labor. This changed with the work of Harry Braverman's Marxist analysis in *Labour and Monopoly Capitalism* in which he condemns management's separation of manual from mental labor.

7. David Harvey, A Brief History of Neo-liberalism (Oxford, Oxford University Press, 2005) as discussed in David Hesmondhalgh's "Neoliberalism, Imperialism and the Media,"
https://www.academia.edu/1534973/Neoliberalism_Imperialism_and_the_Media,
accessed August 11, 2014; also published in The Media and Social Theory, David Hesmondhalgh and Jason Toynbee, eds. (Abingdon, Routledge, 2008).

8. This involves a number of processes, most notably privatisation of government-owned enterprises and institutions, the lifting of restraints on businesses so that they can pursue profit more easily, and the expansion of private ownership and includes paving the way for supposed convergence between telecommunications, media and computers in the 1990s and 2000s.

9. David Hesmondhalgh, "Neo-liberalism, Imperialism and the Media,"
https://www.academia.edu/1534973/Neoliberalism_Imperialism_and_the_Media,
accessed Aug 12, 2014. Also published in *The Media and Social Theory*, David Hesmondhalgh and Jason Toynbee, eds.

(London: Routledge, 2008), 101. Hesmondhalgh says this is one of two factors for neo-liberal marketization in the realm of culture. The second is "the exploitation of understandable anxieties about government intervention in personal, cultural and political expression. As in all of the different realms of economies where neo-liberalism has had an impact, international policy agencies—whether supranational unions of states such as the European Union(EU), trade blocs such as North America Free Trade Agreement (NAFTA) or international trade organizations such as the World Trade Organization (WTO)—have had an important role to play. These changes have contributed to considerable change in the cultural industries since the late 1980s, including the further growth of massive conglomerates, and even greater international flows of culture than before."

10. As Hesmondhalgh explains, for the copyright aspects of TRIPS and their implementation over the last decade suggest that the rise of a new nexus of state and financial power underpinned by neo-liberalism is now becoming increasingly tied to the global governance of symbol production and consumption, with marked effects on how creativity is conceptualized and practiced. There is of course a curious irony here. Neo-liberalism, widely presented by its advocates as a limiting of oppressive government intervention, in the cultural realm as elsewhere actually depends upon state regulation and control. In cultural markets this takes the form of intellectual property statutes, agencies and policing (and other forms too). "Neo-liberalism, Imperialism and the Media."

11. David Hesmondhalgh and Sarah Baker, *Creative Labour: Media Work in Three Cultural Industries*, (London: Routledge, 2010).

12. Wright, 285-6.

13. Harvey, "The Insurgent Architect at Work."

14. In the meanwhile, profit-making organizations that have a social agenda have managed to bend the legal profession to its will by the establishment of the B-corporations and entities called "benefit LLC's," making available to **limited liability companies** the same opportunities afforded to corporations under the Benefit Corporation Law.

15. Wright.

16. See the Graduate School of Architecture, Planning and Preservation at Columbia University' C-BIP studio and its Johannesburg Lab run by Mabel Wilson. See also Danelle Brisco's BIM studios at University of Texas, Austin.

17. For example, at Yale, Keller Easterling's "Launch" and my "Contemporary Labor in Architecture".

18. Given the price tag of their education, they are not fools to expect more return for their investment.

19. I have particular interest in how the academic field of geography turned, almost wholly, to be either Marxist or neo-Marxist/critical. How did this happen? Can it happen to architecture? While Marxism was part of Keith Buchanan's geography work, David Harvey clearly was the most influential in persuading the discipline to think more universally about the conditions it depicted. Those who see themselves as not Marxist geographers but rather "critical" geographers, influenced more by feminism and post-structuralism, still aim at the more socially inclusive agenda. Would that architecture even had this degree of distinction in its disciplinarity.

20. http://changingminds.org/explanations/theories/yale_attitude_change.htm.
Accessed Aug 8, 2014. What I cut out of the 'audience' characteristic... "Lower intelligence and moderate self-esteem helps." Hmmm.

4 On The Impossibility of an Emancipatory Architecture: The Deadlock of Critical Theory, Insurgent Architects, and the Beginning of Politics

1. Kaika, M. 2011, Autistic Architecture: the Fall of the Icon and the Rise of the Serial Object of Architecture, *Environment and Planning D: Society and Space*, 29, 968 – 992.

2. Agamben, G. 2006. Metropolis. In *Metropoli/Moltitudine Seminario Nomade in Tre Atti*. Venice.

3. Marx, K. & F. Engels. 1987. *The German Ideology: Introduction to a Critique of Political Economy* (London: Lawrence and Wishart), 56-57.

4. Wilson, J. & E. Swyngedouw, eds., The Post-Political and its Discontents: Spaces of Depoliticization, Spectres of Radical Politics. Edinburgh: Edinburgh University Press, 2014).

5. Harvey, D. *Spaces of Hope*, (Edinburgh: Edinburgh University Press, 2000).

6. Ibid.

7. Kaika, ibid.

8. Badiou, A., *The Rebirth of History: Times of Riots and Uprisings*. London: Verso, 2012).

9. Kaika, M. & Karaliotas, L., The Spatialization of Democratic Politics: Insights from Indignant Squares, *European Urban and Regional Studies*, 10.1177/0969776414528928 (forthcoming); Karaliotas, L., Staging equality in the squares: Hybrid spaces of political subjectification, *International Journal of Urban and Regional Research* (forthcoming).

10. Swyngedouw, E., Where is the Political? Insurgent Mobilisations and the Incipient 'Return of the Political'. *Space and Polity* 18, 2014, 122-136.

11. Merrifield, A., *The New Urban Question* (London: Pluto Press, 2014).

12. Brenner, N., What is Critical Urban Theory. *City: Analysis of Urban Trends, Culture, Theory, Policy, Action* 13, 2009, 205.

13. Brenner, ibid, 205.

14. Alain Badiou, cited in Peter Hallward, *Badiou—A Subject to Truth*. Minneapolis: University of Minnesota Press, 2003, 394.
15. Badiou, A., Poirier Nicholas—Entretien avec Alain Badiou. *Le Philosophoire*, 9, 1999, 24.
16. Foucault, M., *Security, Territory, Population: Lectures at the Collège de France 1977—1978* (London: Palgrave Macmillan, 2007), 66.
17. Wilson and Swyngedouw, ibid.
18. Rancière, J., Dissenting Words. A Conversation with Jacques Rancière (with Davide Panagia). *Diacritics* 30, 2000, 113-126.
19. Rancière, J., *La Haine de la Démocratie* (Paris: La Fabrique, 2005), 8.
20. Marchart, O, *Post-Foundational Political Thought—Political Difference in Nancy, Lefort, Badiou and Laclau* (Edinburgh: University Press, 2007), 47.
21. Ibid., 47.
22. Rancière, J., "Ten Theses on Politics," in *Theory & Even* 5, 2001, 6.
23. Robson, M., Introduction: Hearing Voices. *Paragraph* 28, 2005, 5.
24. Hallward, ibid, 228.
25. Žižek, S., *The Ticklish Subject: The Absent Centre of Political Ontology* (London: Verso, 1999).
26. Badiou, ibid., 56.
27. Ibid.
28. Swyngedouw, E. & Wilson, J., "There Is No Alternative,",in Wilson J. and E. Swyngedouw, eds., *The Post-Political and its Discontents: Spaces of Depoliticization, Specters of Radical Politics*. Edinburgh: University Press, 2014).

5 The Misery of Theory: On Universality, Contingency, and Truth

1. See http://www.huffingtonpost.com/2011/12/29/young-people-

socialism_n_1175218.html

2. See for example, "What, Me Care? Young Are Less Empathetic" by Jamil Zaki, *Scientific American* (February 2011).

3. See Noam Chomsky, Michel Foucault, *The Chomsky-Foucault Debate: On Human Nature* (The New Press, New York 2006).

4. Bruno Bosteels, *The Actuality of Communism* (London: Verso, 2011)164.

5. On Žižek's theory of the act, see Bosteels, 178.

6. See *The Chomsky-Foucault Debate*.

7. G. W. F. Hegel, *History of Philosophy* (Vol. III) (Omaha NB, University of Nebraska Press 1995). See also https://www.marxists.org/reference/archive/hegel/works/hp/hpfinal.htm#n1

8. Marx, *The German Ideology, Collected Works*, vol. 5 (New York: International Publishers, 1976).

9. Eric Schlosser, "The Prison-Industrial Complex" in *The Atlantic Monthly* (December 1998).

10. Patrick Schumacher, *Digital Hadid: Landscapes in Motion.* Basel: Birkhauser 2003) p. 447.

11. Douglas Spencer, "The New Phantasmagoria: Transcoding the Violence of Fiancial Capitalism" in Nadir Lahiji, ed., *The Missed Encounter of Radical Philosophy with Architecture* (London, Bloomsbury 2014), 82-83.

12. Eyal Weizman, "The Evil Architects Do," in AMOMA/Rem Koolhaas, *Content* (Kohln, Tachen 2004), 60-63.

13. See Zizek, *In Defence of Lost Causes* (London Verso 2008) p. 353 ff.

14. Richard Wolff, *Democracy at Work: a Cure for Capitalism* (Chicago, Haymarket Books 2012) See also http://www.rdwolff.com

15. Luc Boltanski and Eve Chiapello, *The New Spirit of Capitalism* (London and New York, Verso 2005), Part III.

16. Cf. Erin Schell, "The Creativity Bubble: an interview with

Richard Florida" in *Jacobin* (Fall 2014) Double Issue "Paint the Town Red!," 62-72.

17. Pascal Gielen, *Creativity and other Fundamentalisms* (Amsterdam: Mondrian Fund 2013), 47.

18. Gielen, 9.

19. Alex Carey, *Taking the Risk out of Democracy: Corporate Propaganda versus Freedom and Liberty* (Urbana and Chicago: University of Illinois Press, 1995) p. 77-80.

20. Guy Debord, *In Girum Imus Nocte et Consuminur Igni* (Paris, Gallimard 1999) pp. 24-25. My translation.

6 Architecture, Capitalism and the "Autonomy" of the Political

1. Pier Vittorio Aureli, *The Project of Autonomy: Politics and Architecture With and Against Capitalism* (New York: Princeton Architectural Press, 2008), p. 40.

2. Manfredo Tafuri, *Architecture and Utopia: Design and Capitalist Development*, trans. Barbara Luigia La Penta (Cambridge, MA: MIT Press, 1976), p. 182.

3. One might observe that this also has a precursor already internal to the Marxist tradition in the shape of Bernstein's revisionism. Although they try to distance it from simple "reformism", this is acknowledged in *Hegemony and Socialist Strategy* where Laclau and Mouffe credit Bernstein with seeing that "the fragmentation and division characteristic of the new age of capitalism' had to be overcome not 'through changes in the [economic] infrastructure ... [but] through autonomous political intervention. The autonomy of the political from the economic is the true novelty of Bernstein's argument". Ernesto Laclau and Chantal Mouffe, *Hegemony and Socialist Strategy: Towards a Radical Democratic Politics* (London: Verso, 1985), p. 30.

4. Ellen Meiksins Wood, "Capitalism and Human Emancipation", *New Left Review* I/167 (1998), p. 4.

5. For a compelling critique of such attempts to supplement Karl with Carl, see Mark Neocleous, "Friend or Enemy? Reading Schmitt Politically", *Radical Philosophy* 79 (Sept/Oct 1996).

6. Jacques Rancière, *Hatred of Democracy*, trans. Steve Corcoran (London and New York: Verso, 2007), pp. 96-7.

7. See E.P. Thompson, *The Making of the English Working Class* [1963] (London: Penguin, 1991).

8. As Michael Rustin once wrote: "The specific and situated nature of social knowledge [which would of course include a kind of architectural knowledge] should lead to a proper humility in the face of uncertainty, not to the renunciation of understanding as the ground of political practice". Michael Rustin, "Absolute Voluntarism: Critique of a Post-Marxist Concept of Hegemony", *New German Critique* 43 (1988), p. 168. For a more specific critique of Rancière on this point, see Peter Hallward, "Staging Equality: Rancière's Theatrocracy and the Limits of Anarchic Equality", in Gabriel Rockhill and Philip Watts (eds), *Jacques Rancière: History, Politics, Aesthetics* (Durham, NC: Duke University Press, 2009), pp. 154-57.

9. Alberto Toscano, "Burning Dwelling Thinking", *Mute*, online at: http://www.metamute.org/editorial/articles/burning-dwelling-thinking

10. See Fredric Jameson, *Valences of the Dialectic* (London and New York: Verso, 2009).

11. As Rustin points out, Laclau and Mouffe's reference in *Hegemony and Socialist Strategy* to a '"commodification" of social life [that] destroyed previous social relations, replacing them with commodity relations through which the logic of capitalist accumulation penetrated into increasingly numerous spheres' itself relies upon "an explanatory model, which they continue to use even while denying its ontological grounds". See Rustin, "Absolute Voluntarism",

p.170.

12. Slavoj Zizek, "The Parallax of the Critique of Political Economy", online at:

http://www.lacan.com/zizparallax3.htm

This is "Post-Althusserian" in the sense that it both derives from a certain Althusserian attempt to isolate and analyze the "specificity of the political", as is clear in Laclau's early work, *and* ultimately ends up in profound opposition to Althusser himself. This is not, of course, to imply that these various thinkers can thus be thought to pursue essentially compatible positions; something obvious in the case of Laclau and Mouffe's equation of politics with the slow institutional building of hegemony in a form quite at odds with the conceptions of political practice in Badiou or Rancière. Equally, while Rancière and Badiou may possess a shared commitment to an axiom of equality, they, too, actually have very different conceptions of political struggle and organization; a fact which Erik's tendency to move fluidly from citation of one to the other can perhaps too easily efface. Even more so is this the case as regards Zizek, despite the evident debt much of his recent work owes to Badiou, and despite the fact that it is not always easy to identify *any* truly consistent position across his constant stream of writing. Still, it is noticeable that on one of the most significant issues for Erik's piece, and, one would think, for architecture's intersection with politics in general—namely, the role of the State—Zizek takes a markedly different approach to that of either Badiou or Rancière. See Slavoj Zizek, "Foreword: The Dark Matter of Violence, or Putting Terror in Perspective", in Sophie Wahnich, *In Defence of the Terror: Liberty or Death in the French Revolution* (London: Verso, 2012), pp. xi-xxix.

13. Zizek, "The Parallax of the Critique of Political Economy".

14. No doubt Badiou is a slightly more complex case than

Rancière in this respect, but it is still the case that the latter's attempt to refute the accusation that he lacks an "adequate account of the characteristics of contemporary capitalism" by then reducing capitalism to "a regime of gangsters" does not inspire much confidence in the degree to which the problems of political economy are really—or realistically—engaged here. See Alain Badiou, *The Rebirth of History: Times of Riots and Uprisings*, trans. Gregory Elliott (London: Verso, 2012), pp. 7, 12.

15. Susan Buck-Morss, "Envisioning Capital: Political Economy on Display", *Critical Inquiry* 21, 2 (1995), p. 437 (emphasis added).

16. Pier Vittorio Aureli, *The Possibility of an Absolute Architecture* (Cambridge, MA: MIT Press, 2011), pp. 29, ix

17. Fredric Jameson, "Architecture and the Critique of Ideology", in Michael Hays (ed.), *Architecture Theory Since 1968* (Cambridge, MA: MIT Press, 1988), pp. 453, 454.

18. One thinks especially here of Gramsci's notorious assertion that the 1917 Bolshevik Revolution should be understood "as the revolution against Karl Marx's *Capital*". In opposition to the "positivist and naturalist encrustations" that "contaminated" Marx's own thought, Bolshevik politics "sees as the dominant factor in history", according to Gramsci, "not raw economic facts, but man, men in relation to one another, developing through these contacts (civilisation) a collective, social will". Consequently, "events have overcome ideologies. Events have exploded the critical schema determining how the history of Russia would unfold according to the canons of historical materialism". Note, however, that Gramsci's conception of "events" here is far from being a proto-Badiouian messianic eruption, but points to the ways in which *other* historical forces—in this case the First World War—could override narrowly "economic" narratives of development. Antonio Gramsci, "The

Revolution Against 'Capital'", in *Selections from Political Writings 1910-1920* (New York: International Publishers, 1978), pp. 34-35, 36.

19. Famously, Tafuri argues that since the idea of socialism envisaged in the architecture of Red Vienna was an essentially "moral ideal directly confronting the objectivity of the capitalist order", the "autonomy of the political" founded on it becomes a merely subjective voluntarism that could *only be* "symbolic". See Manfredo Tafuri, "Austromarxismo e citta: 'Das rote Wien'" (1971), cited in Aureli, *Project of Autonomy*, p. 50. Notably, Austro-Marxism, to which Tafuri connects this, in some sense anticipates that "autonomy of the political from the economic" sought in *Hegemony and Socialist Strategy*, even if, in other respects, their work remains too tied, for Laclau and Mouffe, to social democratic "orthodoxy".

20. It is worth noting, too, that Tafuri's judgements are often more nuanced in this regard than many imply. The book *Modern Architecture*, written with Dal Co, for example, offers (in 1976) a rather more complex perspective on the potential represented by the then contemporary experiments in urban administration of the Communist Party in "Red Bologna", which, while continuing to stress the "realist" point that "architectural and urbanist proposals cannot be put to the test outside definite political situations, and then only within improved public structures for control", nonetheless suggests that there is a real "historical test" for "the Italian workers' movements" at stake in the "hope that from this new situation may come the realization of the reforms sought for decades". Manfredo Tafuri and Francesco Dal Co, *Modern Architecture*, trans. Robert Erich Wolf; cited Jameson, 'Architecture and the Critique of Ideology', p. 453.

21. Aureli, *The Project of Autonomy*, p. 69.

22. Ibid., p. 44.

23. Ibid., p. 40.

24. Margit Mayer, "Neoliberal Urbanization and the Politics of Contestation", in T. Kaminer, M. Robles-Durán and H. Sohn (eds), *Urban Asymmetries: Studies and Projects on Neoliberal Urbanization* (Rotterdam: 010 Publishers, 2011), pp. xxx, p. 50. The difficult task, of course, as has been attempted by much of the Latin American "new socialism" (if not always very successfully), is to find ways of reciprocally mediating between "grassroots" organizations and state institutions at various levels. Perhaps one of the most inspiring, and aesthetically odd, examples of an "insurgent architecture" to be found in Justin McGuirk's recent book on Latin America is the work of the Túpac Amura movement in Argentina which has been building entire communities for the poor, with its own brick and metal-working factories and employment of the residents as the construction workers, which also combine leftist populism (huge portraits of Che Guevara) with a commitment to forms of luxury one would not associate with social housing (swimming pools and theme park style entertainments). Nonetheless, Túpac Amura's "entire operating budget is based on subsidies it receives from the government for building social housing". As McGuirk notes: "It's incredible to witness what can be achieved with government funding when it's given directly to a well-organized community". Justin McGuirk, *Radical Cities: Across Latin America in Search of a New Architecture* (London and New York: Verso, 2014), pp. 58, 65.

25. See David Cunningham, "The Concept of Metropolis: Philosophy and Urban Form", *Radical Philosophy* 133 (2005), pp. 13-25; and "Metropolitics, or, Architecture and the Contemporary Left", in Nadir Lahiji (ed.), *Architecture Against the Post-Political* (London and New York: Routledge, 2014), pp. 11-30.

26. Massimo Cacciari, *Architecture and Nihilism: On the Philosophy*

of Modern Architecture, trans. Stephen Sartarelli (New Haven: Yale University Press, 1993), pp. 9, 199-200; see also Cunningham, "The Concept of Metropolis".

27. Jameson, *Valences of the Dialectic*, p. 298.

7 Architecture/Agency/Emancipation

1. See my review of K. Michael Hays *Architecture's Desire: Reading the Late Avant-Garde* and Pier Vittorio Aureli's, *The Possibility of an Absolute Architecture*, Volume 17, Issue 1, February 2012, 151-154 and also my essay, "Globalization and the Fate of Theory," in Gevork Hartoonian's edited book, Notes on Critical Architecture (Farnham, England: Ashgate, 2015).

2. If aesthetic autonomy diverts our attention away from the means and methods fueling neo-liberalism and globalization, social autonomy critiques it. Like aesthetic autonomy, social autonomy proposes a retreat from the exchange of goods that serves the powerful global players but it proposes new paradigms of action to resist globalization. Social autonomy, however, has its own conflicting positions and incorporates a number of attributes: a valorization of individual agency, underscoring the belief that the basis for ethical action lies in the autonomy of the actor and the impartiality of his or her reasoning; an anti-consumerist form of practice that spares the subject from the apparatus of commodification; and an emphasis on anti-union, bottom-up organizational mechanisms.

3. The extreme (not even relational) version of this would be Eisenman's belief that the language of architecture is universal and ahistorical, His view probably cannot rightly be called epistemological, since it assumes an a priori condition of apprehension on the part of the apprehender.

4. Much of this analysis of disciplinary autonomy comes from reading article on legal autonomy. A particularly clear essay

is Christopher Tomlin's "How Autonomous is the Law?", Annual Review of Law and Social Science, vol 3: 45-68, December 2007. https://www.deepdyve.com/lp/annual-reviews/how-autonomous-is-law-NGZ8jgaLBm/1. Accessed on December 26, 2014.

5. I wonder if this too is Gail Day's concern when she asked if we aren't recognizing the now outdated definitions that modernism had for "emancipatory" work. Embedded in this is my observation that David and Libero both equate the autonomy/emancipation project with that of modernism, and it makes me wonder if our continual mining of modernism as the site of liberation is *the* biggest problem with critical theory. What if we just look at the present as the present?

6. See Donald Schön, *The Reflective Practitioner: How Professionals Think in Action*, (New York: Basic Books, 1983).

7. Ibid. (no pages given) Tomlin is very insightful in his distinctions which I lean on heavily here.

8. My own particular fascination with BIM is its disruptive capacity that operates within (and seems to be sprung from) the most "professional" and traditionally aesthetic realms of architecture. Its capacity to have architects collaborate with engineers, contractors, and fabricators for efficiency's sake turns into a contractual nightmare thwarting the assignment of risk, itself the source of the contracts that have come to define the profession. Its use of parametrics, initiated in architecture via formally ambitious architects, becomes a system embraced by practitioners uninterested in formal heroics.

9. See the work of Anne Witz, Chris Warhurst and Dennis Nicholson in their "The Labour of Aesthetics and the Aesthetics of Organization," Organization-2003-wits-33-54, http://org.sagepub.com/

(accessed June 1, 2014). They describe the ambiguous class identity of the managers in design offices, who cannot be trusted to advocate for labor or organizational change even if their sentiments might incline them to intellectually support them.

10. This is not to reinforce the blue collar/white collar distinction. Rather, it lays claim to our identify as workers period. And a contractor does deliver buildings, and we don't.

11. Karl Marx, Capital: A Critique of Political Economy, Vol 1, Part II, 605-6. "The quality of the labor is here (in piece-work) controlled by the work itself, which must be of the average perfection if the piece-price is to be paid in full. Piece-wages become, from this point of view, the most fruitful source of reduction of wages and capitalistic cheating.... Given piece-wage, it is naturally the personal interest of the laborer to strain his labour-power as intensely as possible; this enables the capitalist to raise more easily the normal degree of intensity of labor. It is moreover now the personal interest of the laborer to lengthen the working day, since with it his daily or weekly wages rise."

12. Ibid.

13. Manfredo Tafuri, "L'Architecture dans la Boudoir," Oppositions 3, (1974) p. ? .... And also in K. Michael Hays's, Architecture Theory since 1968, (Cambridge, MA: The MIT Press, 1998) 165.

14. See my paper delivered at IOA conference in Newcastle delivered in November 2014 and to be published by Ashgate

15. See Marx on production vs consumption: https://www.marxists.org/archive/marx/works/1857/grundrisse/ch01.htm and the "1859 Preface to A Contribution to the Critique of Political Economy."

8 But What About Left Architecture?

1. Žižek, Slavoj, Žižek! The Documentary Campaign. Zeitgeist Films Ltd, New York, 2005.

2. See, for example, http://www.newstatesman.com/world-affairs/2015/01/slavoj-i-ek-charlie-hebdo-massacre-are-worst-really-full-passionate-intensity —accessed 21/01/2015

3. See http://www.aaschool.ac.uk/VIDEO/lecture.php?ID=2702 —accessed 05/01/2015

4. For a detailed discussion, see Wilson J. and Swyngdouw E., eds., *The Post-Political and its Discontents: Spaces of Depoliticization, Specters of Radical Politics*. Edinburgh University Press, Edinburgh.

5. Swyngedouw E., "'Urban Insurgencies' and the Re-politicization of the Unequal City", in Miraftab F., Salo K and D. Wilson, eds., *Cities and Inequalities in a Global and Transnational World* (New York: Routledge), 173-187.

6. Aureli Pier Vittorio, *The Project of Autonomy: Politics and Architecture Within and Against Capitalism*. Princeton Architectural Press, Princeton, 2008).

7. Ibid., 63.

8. Ricoeur Paul, *History and Truth*. Northwestern University Press, Evanston, 1965).

9. Graham, S., *Cities Under Siege: The New Military Urbanism*. London: Verso, 2011).

10. Žižek, Slavoj, *The Parallax View*. Cambridge: MIT Press, 2006).

11. Kakigianno M. and Rancière J., "A Precarious Dialogue," *Radical Philosophy* 178 (Sept/Oct, 2013), 24.

12. See, for example Gunder M. and Hillier J., *Planning in Ten Words or Less—A Lacanian Entanglement with Spatial Planning* (Farnham: Ashgate, 2009); Swyngedouw E., "Trouble with Nature—Ecology as the New Opium for the People," in

Hillier, J. and P. Healey, eds., *Conceptual Challenges for Planning Theory*. Farnham: Aldershot, 2010), 299-320.

13. Harvey David, *Rebel Cities—From the Right to the City to the Urban Revolution* (London: Verso, 2012); Merrifield A., *The Politics of the Encounter: Urban Theory and Protest under Planetary Urbanization*. University of Georgia Press, Atlanta, 2013).

14. Beverungen A., Murtola A.M. and Schwarts G., "The Communism of Capital," *Ephemera* 13(3), 2013.

15. Badiou Alain, *The Communist Hypothesis*. London: Verso, 2010).

16. Žižek, Slavoj, "Nature and its Discontents," *SubStance* 37(3), 2008, 37-72.

17. Levine R.M., *Vale of Tears: Revisiting the Canudos Massacre in Northeastern Brazil, 1893-1897* (University of California Press, Berkeley, 1995).

18. Vargas Llosa M., *The War of the End of the World* (Faber and Faber, New York, 2004).

19. Mann G., "A Negative Geography of Necessity," *Antipode* 40(5), 2008, 921-934.

9 The Project of Emancipation, the Communist Hypothesis, and A Plea for *The Platonism of Architecture*

1. See Alain Badiou, 'Must the communist Hypothesis be Abandoned?' in *The Meaning of Sarkozy* (London and New York: 2008), 97.

2. Alain Badiou, *The Meaning of Sarkozy* (London and New York: 2008), 99.

3. Ibid., 99-100.

4. Ibid., 100.

5. Ibid., 101.

6. Ibid., 102.

7. See Bruno Bosteels, The Actuality of Communism (London and New York: Verso, 2011), 6.

8. Ibid., 8-9, also see Isabelle Garo, 'le communisme vu d'ici ou lapolitique au sens plein,' in *Contre-Temps: Revue de critique communiste* 4 (2009), 40.

9. Badiou, *The Meaning of Sarkozy*, ibid., 113.

10. In *The Meaning of Sarkozy*, ibid., 113-14.

11. Alain Badiou, "The Idea of Communism,' in Costas Douzinas and Slavoj Zizek, ed., *The Idea of Communism* (London and New york: Verso, 2010), 8., also see, Bosteels, ibid., 35-36.

12. Bosteels, ibid., 37.

13. Ibid., 37.

14. Ibid., 39.

15. Ibid.. Bosteels further cites Zizek: 'Hegel always insists on the absolute primacy of actuality: true, the search for the "condition of possibility" abstracts from the actual, calls it into question, in order to (re)constitute a rational basis; yet in all these ruminations actuality is presupposed as something given', ibid, 39-40, also see Slavoj Zizek, *Tarrying with the Negative: Kant, Hegel, and the Critique of Ideology* (Durham: Duke University Press, 1993), 157.

16. Costas Douzinas and Slavoj Zizek, eds., *The Idea of Communism* (London and New York: Verso, 2010), vii.

17. Ibid.,

18. Ibid., ix.

19. Veronique Bergen, 'Un communisme des singulariteés,' in *ContreTemps: Revue de critique communiste* 4 (2009), 17., quoted in Bosteels, ibid., 36.

20. Bosteels, ibid., 38.

21. Ibid., 39.

22. Ibid.

23. Bosteels elaborates on this term discussed by Alain Badiou and Jacques Ranciere; for more see Bosteels, ibid.

24. For this and what follows see Gerald A. Press, *Plato: A Gide for the Perplex* (London: Continuum, 2007), 51.

25. Ibid., 31.

26. Ibid., 40.

27. Ibid., 84.

28. Ibid.

29. Gilles Deleuze, *Difference and Repetition*, trans. Paul Patton (New York: Columbia University Press, 1994), 66.

30. See Livingston, ibid., 107.

31. Deleuze, *Difference and Repetition*, ibid., xix.

32. Livingston, ibid., 107.

33. Quoted in ibid., 4.

34. Ibid.

35. Quoted in Livingston, Ibid., 9.

36. Quoted in Peter Hallward, *Badiou, Subject to Truth* (Minneapolis: University of Minnesota Press, 2003)., 5.

37. Hallward, ibid.

38. See *The Communist Hypothesis*, ibid., 235.

39. Ibid.

40. Ibid., 237.

41. Ibid., 239.

42. Ibid., N. 8, 240

43. Ibid., 249-50. In the footnote for above passage Badiou writes: 'Those who have "no name," those who have "no part," and ultimately , in all current political actions, the organizational role of the workers "without papers" are all part of a negative, or rather stripped down, view of the human terrain of emancipatory politics. Jacques Rancière, starting in particular with his in-depth study of theses themes in the nineteenth century, has specifically highlighted, in the philosophical field the implications for democracy of not belonging to a dominant societal category. This idea actually goes back at least as far as to the Marx of the *Manuscript of 1844*, who defined the proletariat as generic humanity, since it does not itself possess any of the properties by which the bourgeoisie defines (respectable, or normal, or "well-adjusted," as we would say today) Man,'

ibid.249.

44. See Alain Badiou, 'The History of the Communist Hypothesis and Its Present Moment,' in *The Meaning of Sarkozy*, ibid.

45. Quoted in *Jacques Rancière: History, Politics, Aesthetics*, eds., Gabriel Rockhill and Philip Watts (Durham and London: Duke University Press, 2009), 3. See also, Jacques Rancière, *Althusser's Lesson*, trans., Emiliano Battista (London: Continuum, 2011).

46. Jacques Rancière, *Disagreement: Politics and Philosophy* (Minneapolis: University of Minnesota Press, 1999),15. Rancière further writes:' The party of the poor embodies nothing other than politics itself as the setting-up of a part of those have no part. Symmetrically, the party of rich embodies nothing other than the antipolitical. From Athens in the fifth century B.C. up until our own governments, the party of the rich has only ever said on thing, which is most precisely the negation of politics: there is no part of those who have no part,' ibid., 14.

Afterword

1. Karl Marx, *Theses on Feuerbach* (1845/1888), XI, online at https://www.marxists.org/archive/marx/works/1845/theses/theses.htm.

2. Walter Benjamin, "Surrealism: The Last Snapshot of the European Intelligentsia," in *Reflections: Essays, Aphorisms, Autobiographical Writings*, trans. Edmund Jephcott (New York: Harcourt Brace Jovanovich, 1979), 192.

3. Luc Boltanski and Eve Chiapello, *The New Spirit of Capitalism* (London: Verso, 2005).

4. Manfredo Tafuri, *The Sphere and the Labyrinth: Avant-Gardes and Architecture from Piranesi to the 1970s*, trans. Pellegrino d'Acierno and Robert Connally (Cambridge, MA: MIT Press, 1986), 8.

5. Ibid., 303.
6. See Joan Ockman, "Venice and New York," special issue on "The Historical Project of Manfredo Tafuri," *Casabella* 619–620 (January–February 1995), 56–67.
7. See the interview with Koolhaas conducted by Jennifer Sigler in 2000 in *Index* Magazine, online at http://www.indexmagazine.com/interviews/rem_koolhaas.shtml.
8. Hans Magnus Enzensberger, "A Critique of Political Ecology," *New Left Review*, March–April 1974, 30.
9. See, for example, David Harvey, "The Fetish of Technology: Causes and Consequences," *Macalester International* 13, no. 1 (2003), 3–30; online at http://digitalcommons.macalester.edu/macintl/vol13/iss1/7/.
10. Enzensberger, "A Critique of Political Ecology," 13.
11. Olinde Rodrigues, "L'artiste, le savant et l'industriel. Dialogue," in Léon Halévy and Henri Saint-Simon, *Opinions littéraires, philosophiques et industrielles* (Paris: Galérie Bossange Père, 1825), 341, 347. The original reads: "C'est nous, artistes, qui vous servirons d'avant-garde: la puissance des arts est en effet la plus immédiate et la plus rapide. ... Quelle plus belle destinée pour les arts, que d'exercer sur la société une puissance positive, un veritable sacerdoce, et de s'élancer en avant de toutes les facultés intellectuelles, à l'époque de leur plus grand développement!" Online at https://archive.org/details/opinionslittrai00saingoog.

Contemporary culture has eliminated both the concept of the public and the figure of the intellectual. Former public spaces – both physical and cultural – are now either derelict or colonized by advertising. A cretinous anti-intellectualism presides, cheerled by expensively educated hacks in the pay of multinational corporations who reassure their bored readers that there is no need to rouse themselves from their interpassive stupor. The informal censorship internalized and propagated by the cultural workers of late capitalism generates a banal conformity that the propaganda chiefs of Stalinism could only ever have dreamt of imposing. Zer0 Books knows that another kind of discourse – intellectual without being academic, popular without being populist – is not only possible: it is already flourishing, in the regions beyond the striplit malls of so-called mass media and the neurotically bureaucratic halls of the academy. Zer0 is committed to the idea of publishing as a making public of the intellectual. It is convinced that in the unthinking, blandly consensual culture in which we live, critical and engaged theoretical reflection is more important than ever before.

ZERO BOOKS

If this book has helped you to clarify an idea, solve a problem or extend your knowledge, you may like to read more titles from Zero Books. Recent bestsellers are:

Capitalist Realism Is there no alternative?
Mark Fisher
An analysis of the ways in which capitalism has presented itself as the only realistic political-economic system.
Paperback: November 27, 2009 978-1-84694-317-1 $14.95 £7.99.
eBook: July 1, 2012 978-1-78099-734-6 $9.99 £6.99.

The Wandering Who? A study of Jewish identity politics
Gilad Atzmon
An explosive unique crucial book tackling the issues of Jewish Identity Politics and ideology and their global influence.
Paperback: September 30, 2011 978-1-84694-875-6 $14.95 £8.99.
eBook: September 30, 2011 978-1-84694-876-3 $9.99 £6.99.

Clampdown Pop-cultural wars on class and gender
Rhian E. Jones
Class and gender in Britpop and after, and why 'chav' is a feminist issue.
Paperback: March 29, 2013 978-1-78099-708-7 $14.95 £9.99.
eBook: March 29, 2013 978-1-78099-707-0 $7.99 £4.99.

The Quadruple Object
Graham Harman
Uses a pack of playing cards to present Harman's metaphysical system of fourfold objects, including human access, Heidegger's indirect causation, panpsychism and ontography.
Paperback: July 29, 2011 978-1-84694-700-1 $16.95 £9.99.

Weird Realism Lovecraft and Philosophy
Graham Harman
As Hölderlin was to Martin Heidegger and Mallarmé to Jacques
Derrida, so is H.P. Lovecraft to the Speculative Realist philoso-
phers.
Paperback: September 28, 2012 978-1-78099-252-5 $24.95 £14.99.
eBook: September 28, 2012 978-1-78099-907-4 $9.99 £6.99.

Sweetening the Pill or How We Got Hooked on Hormonal Birth
Control
Holly Grigg-Spall
Is it really true? Has contraception liberated or oppressed women?
Paperback: September 27, 2013 978-1-78099-607-3 $22.95 £12.99.
eBook: September 27, 2013 978-1-78099-608-0 $9.99 £6.99.

Why Are We The Good Guys? Reclaiming Your Mind From The
Delusions Of Propaganda
David Cromwell
A provocative challenge to the standard ideology that Western
power is a benevolent force in the world.
Paperback: September 28, 2012 978-1-78099-365-2 $26.95 £15.99.
eBook: September 28, 2012 978-1-78099-366-9 $9.99 £6.99.

The Truth about Art Reclaiming quality
Patrick Doorly
The book traces the multiple meanings of art to their various
sources, and equips the reader to choose between them.
Paperback: August 30, 2013 978-1-78099-841-1 $32.95 £19.99.

Bells and Whistles More Speculative Realism
Graham Harman
In this diverse collection of sixteen essays, lectures, and interviews
Graham Harman lucidly explains the principles of Speculative
Realism, including his own object-oriented philosophy.

Paperback: November 29, 2013 978-1-78279-038-9 $26.95 £15.99.
eBook: November 29, 2013 978-1-78279-037-2 $9.99 £6.99.

Towards Speculative Realism: Essays and Lectures Essays and Lectures
Graham Harman
These writings chart Harman's rise from Chicago sportswriter to co founder of one of Europe's most promising philosophical movements: Speculative Realism.
Paperback: November 26, 2010 978-1-84694-394-2 $16.95 £9.99.
eBook: January 1, 1970 978-1-84694-603-5 $9.99 £6.99.

Meat Market Female flesh under capitalism
Laurie Penny
A feminist dissection of women's bodies as the fleshy fulcrum of capitalist cannibalism, whereby women are both consumers and consumed.
Paperback: April 29, 2011 978-1-84694-521-2 $12.95 £6.99.
eBook: May 21, 2012 978-1-84694-782-7 $9.99 £6.99.

Translating Anarchy The Anarchism of Occupy Wall Street
Mark Bray
An insider's account of the anarchists who ignited Occupy Wall Street.
Paperback: September 27, 2013 978-1-78279-126-3 $26.95 £15.99.
eBook: September 27, 2013 978-1-78279-125-6 $6.99 £4.99.

One Dimensional Woman
Nina Power
Exposes the dark heart of contemporary cultural life by examining pornography, consumer capitalism and the ideology of women's work.
Paperback: November 27, 2009 978-1-84694-241-9 $14.95 £7.99.
eBook: July 1, 2012 978-1-78099-737-7 $9.99 £6.99.

Dead Man Working

Carl Cederstrom, Peter Fleming

An analysis of the dead man working and the way in which capital is now colonizing life itself.

Paperback: May 25, 2012 978-1-78099-156-6 $14.95 £9.99.

eBook: June 27, 2012 978-1-78099-157-3 $9.99 £6.99.

Unpatriotic History of the Second World War

James Heartfield

The Second World War was not the Good War of legend. James Heartfield explains that both Allies and Axis powers fought for the same goals - territory, markets and natural resources.

Paperback: September 28, 2012 978-1-78099-378-2 $42.95 £23.99.

eBook: September 28, 2012 978-1-78099-379-9 $9.99 £6.99.

Find more titles at www.zero-books.net